CW00685821

A Vegan Taste of North Africa

Other cookbooks by Linda Majzlik published by Jon Carpenter

Party Food for Vegetarians
Vegan Dinner Parties
Vegan Baking
Vegan Barbecues and Buffets
A Vegan Taste of the Caribbean
A Vegan Taste of Italy
A Vegan Taste of India
A Vegan Taste of Mexico
A Vegan Taste of the Middle East
A Vegan Taste of Greece
A Vegan Taste of France

A Vegan Taste
of
North Africa

Linda Majzlik

Jon Carpenter

Our books may be ordered from bookshops or (post free) from
Jon Carpenter Publishing, Alder House, Market Street, Charlbury,
England OX7 3PH

Credit card orders can be phoned or faxed to 01689 870437
or 01608 811969

First published in 2003 by
Jon Carpenter Publishing
Alder House, Market Street, Charlbury, Oxfordshire OX7 3PH
☎ 01608 811969

© Linda Majzlik 2003

Illustrations by Amanda Henriques © 2003

The right of Linda Majzlik to be identified as author of this work has been
asserted in accordance with the Copyright, Design and Patents Act 1988

All rights reserved. No part of this publication may be reproduced, stored in a
retrieval system or transmitted in any form or by any means electronic,
mechanical, photocopying or otherwise without the prior permission in
writing of the publisher

ISBN 1 897766 83 1

Printed in England by J. W. Arrowsmith Ltd., Bristol

CONTENTS

Sauces, dressings and condiments

Desserts

Baking

Drinks

INTRODUCTION

THE FIVE ADJOINING COUNTRIES OF MOROCCO, ALGERIA, TUNISIA, LIBYA AND Egypt are the most northerly in Africa, the world's second largest continent. Together they occupy a vast area, with each individual country's coastline bordering the Mediterranean Sea. As most of the region consists of scrub, semi-desert, desert or mountains, fertile growing areas are scarce. They are limited to coastal plains, which enjoy a Mediterranean climate, and the valley and delta of the Nile in Egypt, where an extensive irrigation system allows crop cultivation. A wide variety of crops are grown in these areas, including wheat, barley, millet, rice, olives, nuts, vegetables and citrus and other fruits. Palm trees thrive in the more arid areas and produce a huge crop of dates, a favourite food used both as a snack and as an ingredient in all the countries.

Along with all the other African nations, those in the north have had a long and chequered history and the original inhabitants of a large part of the region, the Berbers, were frequently routed by successive waves of invaders, who brought with them new religions, cultures, styles of cooking and ingredients. Until recently the North African countries were under European control and today, as well as by religious dietary customs, much of the cuisine of the region has been greatly influenced by an interesting and exotic mixture of flavours and ingredients from Europe as well as from the East, a legacy of the past invaders.

Modern day North African cooks prepare dishes from recipes that are more often than not passed down through the generations by word of mouth rather than in any written form. Fresh vegetables, fruits, herbs and spices are bought from stalls piled high with produce in the many colourful and lively open-air market places. Most herbs are used fresh and spices are bought whole for grinding at home as and when required. North Africans take great pride in their hospitality and communal eating with family and friends is a common feature in the region. At these gatherings guests are invited to help themselves to a varied selection of dishes, which are usually arranged on low tables. Bread is a very important staple and revered accompaniment and is served at every meal. The breaking of the bread by the host is a signal to the guests that they may begin their meal.

Although all these countries have their own particular favourites, seasonings and signature dishes, richly-flavoured aromatic stews and tagines, piled high on a bed of couscous, are commonly served all over the region. Meals are often rounded off with simple fruit salads flavoured with flower waters or rich pastries or puddings served with mint tea. Between-meal sweet and savoury snacks are very popular and these are also served with mint tea or with strong black coffee.

With the emphasis on basic, wholesome and nutritious ingredients, imaginatively combined with herbs and spices, North African cuisine offers the vegan cook the perfect opportunity to experiment with this exciting, colourful and vibrant style of cooking.

THE VEGAN NORTH AFRICAN STORECUPBOARD

NORTH AFRICAN COOKS SHOP IN VIBRANT AND BUSTLING MARKET PLACES FOR fresh seasonal fruits and vegetables and combine these with storecupboard basics to create a diverse range of distinctively flavoured dishes.

Almonds Rich in protein, vitamins in the B complex, vitamin E and calcium, almonds are used in numerous sweet and savoury recipes. Their flavour is enhanced if lightly toasted.

Apricots Dried apricots are used in a variety of dishes, both sweet and savoury, and are also blended to make delicious drinks. Apricots are rich in iron, fibre, vitamins and minerals. Choose plump, unsulphured varieties for the best flavour.

Barley Grown in Morocco, Tunisia and Algeria, barley provides a staple food in parts of the region. Whole or pot barley is more wholesome than pearl as it has not lost important nutrients in the milling process. Barley can be served as a grain dish as an alternative to rice or couscous, added to soups and stews or mixed with other ingredients and served cold as a salad.

Beans Many varieties are used throughout the region, with blackeye, red kidney, haricot and fava being some of the most popular. All beans are a good source of protein, fibre and minerals. They can be cooked in bulk as they freeze successfully.

Breadcrumbs Used mainly to bind or coat savoury mixtures, breadcrumbs can easily be made by whizzing chunks of bread in a food processor or nutmill. Breadcrumbs can be stored in the freezer and used from frozen.

Bulgar wheat Made from crushed, cooked and dried wheat berries which have had their bran layer removed, bulgar simply needs to be rehydrated in liquid

THE VEGAN NORTH AFRICAN STORECUPBOARD

NORTH AFRICAN COOKS SHOP IN VIBRANT AND BUSTLING MARKET PLACES FOR fresh seasonal fruits and vegetables and combine these with storecupboard basics to create a diverse range of distinctively flavoured dishes.

Almonds Rich in protein, vitamins in the B complex, vitamin E and calcium, almonds are used in numerous sweet and savoury recipes. Their flavour is enhanced if lightly toasted.

Apricots Dried apricots are used in a variety of dishes, both sweet and savoury, and are also blended to make delicious drinks. Apricots are rich in iron, fibre, vitamins and minerals. Choose plump, unsulphured varieties for the best flavour.

Barley Grown in Morocco, Tunisia and Algeria, barley provides a staple food in parts of the region. Whole or pot barley is more wholesome than pearl as it has not lost important nutrients in the milling process. Barley can be served as a grain dish as an alternative to rice or couscous, added to soups and stews or mixed with other ingredients and served cold as a salad.

Beans

before serving, although it can also be cooked pilaff-style with other ingredients.

Capers The small green flower buds from a spiny trailing shrub, capers have a piquant taste and are sold preserved in either vinegar or brine. They are used as an ingredient and as a garnish.

'Cheese' Some Mediterranean-inspired dishes contain 'cheese' and cheddar-style substitutes made from soya have been used in the recipes here.

Chickpeas Creamy, nutty flavoured peas which combine well with any other ingredient and are a good source of protein, fibre, vitamins and minerals. They are used in soups and stews or mashed to make little savouries or spreads.

Chocolate Egyptians are very fond of chocolate and use it regularly in various cakes and drinks. An ever-increasing range of vegan chocolate bars is available from supermarkets and health food shops.

Couscous A fundamental and staple ingredient, couscous is made from fine particles of semolina which are processed into tiny, grain-like pellets. Wholewheat and refined versions are available. It is plainly cooked, flavoured with herbs or spices or mixed with other ingredients and forms an essential accompaniment for stews and casseroles. Couscous is also used in salads and puddings and for stuffing vegetables.

Dates The date palm is a common sight in all North African countries and dates are naturally a favourite ingredient in both sweet and savoury dishes. Fresh dates are often split, filled with ground nuts and served as a snack or appetiser. Dates for cooking are sold pitted and loose or pitted and compressed into blocks. For stuffing or using whole in fruit salads boxed dessert dates are best.

Filo pastry Widely used all over the region in sweet and savoury recipes, filo pastry is made from flour, salt and water, but it is best bought frozen or chilled, as it is difficult and time-consuming to make. The sheets need to be brushed with either melted margarine for sweet recipes or olive oil for savoury recipes before baking in the oven. However, many filo-encased North African pastries are fried rather than baked and these do not have to be brushed with oil before cooking.

Flower waters Both rose and orange flower waters are used as essential flavourings in desserts, cakes, biscuits and drinks. Beware of imitations –

authentic flower waters are distilled from real flowers and not chemically produced.

Ginger, fresh For a more robust ginger flavour the fresh root is sometimes used in preference to the dried ground variety. To store fresh root ginger, cut it into useable-sized pieces, wrap in kitchen foil and freeze.

Ginger, stem Available in jars preserved in sugar syrup, stem ginger can be chopped and added to fresh and dried fruit salads.

Green tea Reputedly first introduced into the region in the 18th century, green tea leaves are favoured for steeping with fresh mint to make mint tea. As well as being a reviving drink, green tea contains a powerful group of antioxidants and has a lower caffeine content than black tea.

Ground rice White rice which has been milled to a grainy powder, ground rice is combined with other ingredients to made sweet rice puddings.

Harissa A hot chilli-based paste widely found in Morocco, Tunisia and Algeria, harissa is used to add its distinctive flavour to soups, stews and sauces or is spread neat onto bread as a topping. It is available ready-made in jars, but it can easily be made at home (see page 90).

Herbs Fresh herbs are preferred and these are sold alongside fresh vegetables in the market place. However, dried herbs, especially mint, are sometimes used when a more intense flavour is required.

Coriander A uniquely flavoured herb and an essential ingredient in North African cuisine. It is by far the most popular herb in the region and is widely used in all kinds of savoury dishes and for garnishing.

Dill This feathery-leafed herb has a distinctive aniseed flavour which combines very well with mint. Dill also has a natural affinity with green vegetables, potatoes and carrots.

Marjoram This tiny-leafed herb has a very distinct, aromatic flavour and is used in Mediterranean-style dishes.

Mint An essential herb, not only for making mint tea but for numerous other dishes, where it is often used in combination with other herbs. Dried mint is sometimes used for a stronger flavour.

Oregano An attractive, small-leafed herb which goes well with tomatoes. It is often combined with marjoram in Mediterranean-style dishes.

Parsley A universally popular herb, the flat leaf variety is preferred and this is used liberally in savoury dishes and for garnishing.

Thyme A small-leafed highly aromatic herb which combines well with lemon and is used with other herbs to make marinades and dressings.

Lemon juice With citrus fruits being widely grown in the region, fresh lemon juice is used in numerous savoury dishes to give a desired sharp flavour.

Lentils All lentils are a rich source of protein, fibre, vitamins and minerals and red, green and brown varieties are used to make soups, stews and salads.

Millet A crop which thrives in dry, hot climates and can grow in poor soils, which makes it ideal for cultivating in parts of North Africa where other crops fail to grow. Millet has a delicate, nutty flavour and is rich in protein and iron. It is used plainly cooked or mixed with other ingredients as an accompaniment to stews and casseroles.

Olive oil An essential ingredient for dressings and marinades and also for cooking. Olive oil is uniquely flavoured and has no substitute. The most expensive kind, extra virgin oil, is considered to be the best. Although production rates vary depending on the weather conditions, Tunisia is usually the fourth largest producer of olive oil in the world.

Olives Widely grown in the fertile coastal plains of Morocco, Tunisia, Algeria and Libya, olives are enjoyed as a snack or appetiser or used as an ingredient or garnish.

Pasta Although most pasta is simply made from durum wheat and water, some varieties contain egg so always read the ingredients label. Soups containing pasta are especially popular in Libya and stews and casseroles are often served on a bed of pasta there.

Pine kernels These tiny fragrant nuts have a sweet creamy taste and are the seeds of a type of pine tree that is native to the Mediterranean area. Their flavour is enhanced if they are lightly toasted and they are used as a garnish and as an ingredient.

Pistachio nuts Light green coloured, flavourful nuts which are sold in their split shells or ready-shelled, either salted or unsalted. The unsalted variety is used in both savoury and sweet recipes and bowls of nuts are often served as appetisers or for dessert.

Preserved lemons Available bottled in specialist shops and delicatessen or easily made at home (see page 91). To use the lemons remove the inner fleshy part, then wash the peel thoroughly to remove any salt, chop or slice it finely and add to savoury dishes to give a fragrant lemony flavour. Alternatively, use the peel as a garnish or serve separately as a condiment.

Prunes The dried fruit of a black-skinned plum, prunes contain iron, calcium and vitamins and are used in both sweet and savoury dishes.

Rice A staple food, especially in Egypt where it is grown in the Nile valley. White and brown long grain varieties are served plainly cooked or mixed with other ingredients.

Semolina A nutritious and versatile meal made from durum wheat, semolina is used in various cake, biscuit and pudding recipes or mixed with flour to make a grainy-textured pastry.

Spices For strength of flavour and freshness, North African cooks prefer to use whole spices and grind them in a mortar when required.

Aniseed With a very distinctive licorice flavour, aniseed is often used to flavour breads.

Black pepper A universally popular seasoning for savoury dishes. Freshly ground black peppercorns are preferred.

Caraway seeds Caraway seeds look similar to cumin seeds, but taste very differently. They have a sweet, slightly aniseedy flavour which combines very well with carrots.

Cardamom This pine-fragranced spice is available in three forms – as pods, seeds or ground. The pods vary in colour but it is generally agreed that the green variety is most flavourful and aromatic. The seeds are commonly ground and used to flavour strong black coffee.

Cayenne pepper The dried fruit of a hot red pepper, deep red in colour and very pungent. Cayenne is used to add 'heat' to a dish.

Cinnamon Used both as sticks and ground, cinnamon has a warm, comforting sweet flavour and is used extensively in sweet and savoury dishes.

Cloves Dried buds of an evergreen tree which are valued for their anaesthetic and antiseptic properties. Whole cloves are often used to flavour spicy grain dishes and fruit salads, while ground cloves are used in various cakes and pastries.

Coriander The dried seed of a plant which belongs to the parsley family. Coriander seeds have a mild, sweet orangey flavour which is enhanced when the seeds are crushed.

Cumin Used as both whole seeds and ground, cumin has a strong earthy flavour and is regularly used in all kinds of savoury dishes.

Ginger The dried ground root has a strong, spicy but sweet flavour and adds a more mellow gingery taste than the fresh variety. It is often combined with turmeric and paprika in Moroccan stews and soups.

Nutmeg The large, aromatic, sweet and spicy seed of an evergreen tropical tree, nutmeg is used sparingly in savoury and sweet dishes.

Paprika A dried and ground sweet red pepper which adds colour and a mild, sweet flavour to savoury dishes, especially those containing tomatoes.

Saffron This most expensive of all spices, saffron is made from the dried stigmas of a variety of crocus. Luckily, only a small amount is needed to provide a yellow colour and a pungent, slightly bitter, yet aromatic taste. It is used in particular to add colour and flavour to couscous and rice.

Turmeric A bright-yellow spice which is the powdered rhizome of a plant belonging to the ginger family. It is valued for its anti-bacterial properties and adds colour and a distinctive earthy pungency to numerous savoury dishes.

Sun-dried tomatoes Available dry, for reconstituting in water, or preserved in olive oil, ready to use, sun-dried tomatoes have a unique and intense flavour. A sun-dried tomato paste is also available, which has a stronger, richer flavour than tomato purée.

Soya milk Unsweetened soya milk has been used in both sweet and savoury recipes.

Sunflower oil This light, neutral-tasting oil is often used for breads, cakes and pastries and for frying sweet and savoury goods.

Tahini A thick nutritious paste made from ground sesame seeds, tahini is rich in protein, calcium and B vitamins. It adds a distinctive flavour and richness to savoury spreads or can simply be used neat as a topping on bread. Two varieties of tahini are available – dark, which is made from roasted sesame seeds and has a slightly bitter flavour, or light, which is more creamy and is the one used in the recipes here.

Textured vegetable protein A nutritious and versatile soya product which readily absorbs the flavours of other ingredients. The natural minced variety is used here in various savoury dishes.

Tinned tomatoes Sometimes used in preference to fresh tomatoes if a stronger tomato flavour is required.

Tomato purée Used to strengthen the flavour of and add colour to tomato-based dishes.

Vegetable stock Used in a variety of savoury recipes, home-made vegetable stock gives a more authentic flavour than stock cubes. It can be made in bulk and frozen in measured quantities. Peel and chop a selection of vegetables such as carrots, celery, courgettes, peppers, onion and potato. Put them in a pan and add a couple of chopped garlic cloves, a few sprigs of parsley and a bay leaf. Cover with water and bring to the boil. Cover the pan and simmer for 30 minutes, then strain.

Vinegar Balsamic and red and white wine vinegars are used in dressings for salads, charmoulas and sauces.

Walnuts A rich source of polyunsaturated fats, studies have shown that walnuts have positive health benefits by helping to lower cholesterol levels. They are used as an ingredient and as a garnish in various sweet and savoury recipes.

Yeast Easy-blend dried yeast is used in the recipes here. It does not need to be reconstituted in liquid.

Yoghurt Regularly used in North Africa both as an ingredient in sweet and savoury recipes or simply as a garnish for savoury dishes. Plain soya yoghurt is an excellent substitute.

SNACKS AND STARTERS

At larger gatherings and special family get-togethers, a selection of starters is usually offered. Other dishes that could be included here are bowls of nuts, dates, salads and vegetables. Savoury snacks, either made at home or bought from the multitude of food stalls in the colourful and exotic market places, are eaten at any time of day. A Tunisian speciality, brik, is traditionally made from paper-thin sheets of pastry made from ground semolina, but filo pastry makes a very good substitute for this. Countless variations of brik are made and savoury and sweet fillings are equally popular. Stuffed pitta breads are a favourite snack food across the whole of the region and leftover food is usually kept to use as fillings for these.

AUBERGINE AND ALMOND KEFTAS
(MAKES APPROX. 16)

8oz/225g aubergine, finely chopped

3oz/75g ground almonds

3oz/75g breadcrumbs

1oz/25g natural minced textured vegetable protein

5 fl.oz/150ml water

2 tablespoons olive oil

1 onion, peeled and grated

1 rounded tablespoon finely chopped fresh parsley

1 rounded tablespoon finely chopped fresh coriander

1 rounded teaspoon ground cumin

¼ teaspoon ground cinnamon

black pepper

flour

extra olive oil

Fry the aubergine and onion in the 2 tablespoonfuls of oil for 10 minutes, stirring frequently to prevent sticking. Add the vegetable protein, water, parsley, coriander, cumin and cinnamon and season with black pepper. Stir well and bring to the boil, then cover and simmer, stirring frequently, for 5-10 minutes until the liquid has been absorbed. Remove from the heat and add the ground almonds and breadcrumbs. Add a little flour to bind, then take rounded dessertspoonfuls of the mixture and with damp hands mould into small sausage shapes. Put these in a greased baking dish and brush with olive oil. Bake in a preheated oven at 180°C/350°F/Gas mark 4 for about 25 minutes until golden brown. Serve with a salad garnish.

SAVOURY RICE BRIK (MAKES 6)

6 sheets filo pastry (of approx. 5 x 18 inches/13 x 46cm)

olive oil

4oz/100g long grain rice

4oz/100g red pepper, finely chopped

4oz/100g carrot, scraped and grated

1 onion, peeled and finely chopped

1 garlic clove, crushed

1oz/25g walnuts, finely chopped

½oz/15g raisins

10 fl.oz/300ml vegetable stock or water

1 tablespoon olive oil

1 inch/2.5cm cinnamon stick, crumbled

1 teaspoon ground cumin

½ teaspoon turmeric

¼ teaspoon cayenne pepper

black pepper

ground cinnamon

Fry the red pepper, carrot, onion and garlic in the tablespoonful of oil for 5 minutes. Add the cinnamon, cumin, turmeric and cayenne pepper and stir around for 30 seconds, then add the rice, raisins, and vegetable stock and season with black pepper. Stir well and bring to the boil, cover and simmer gently until the liquid has been absorbed. Remove from the heat, stir in the walnuts and allow to cool.

Place the filo sheets on a flat surface and divide the filling equally between them, putting it neatly in an oblong shape at one end of each sheet. Fold the two long edges of pastry over to enclose the sides of the filling, then carefully roll each brik up to make a small parcel. Shallow fry these in hot olive oil for a few minutes on each side until golden. Drain on kitchen paper and sprinkle lightly with ground cinnamon before serving.

EGYPTIAN TA'AMIA (SERVES 6)

1lb/450g cooked chickpeas, mashed

2oz/50g breadcrumbs

1 onion, peeled

4 garlic cloves

2 tablespoons lemon juice

2 rounded tablespoons finely chopped fresh coriander

1 rounded teaspoon ground cumin

1 rounded teaspoon ground coriander

½ teaspoon turmeric

black pepper

olive oil for frying

Mince the onion with the garlic and put in a mixing bowl with the chickpeas, breadcrumbs, lemon juice, fresh coriander, ground cumin and coriander and turmeric. Season with black pepper and combine thoroughly. Take rounded dessertspoonfuls of the mixture and shape into balls in the palm of the hand. Flatten each ball slightly, then fry them in olive oil for a few minutes on each side until browned. Drain on kitchen paper and serve warm with a salad garnish.

ROASTED AUBERGINE SPREAD (SERVES 4)

1½lb/675g aubergine

2 garlic cloves, crushed

2 rounded tablespoons light tahini

2 dessertspoons lemon juice

1 dessertspoon olive oil

½ teaspoon ground cumin

black pepper

extra olive oil

Halve the aubergine lengthwise and make a few slits in the skin with a sharp knife. Brush with olive oil and place under a hot grill, turning occasionally until the flesh is tender. Allow to cool slightly, then carefully remove the skins. Mash the flesh, add the remaining ingredients and mix thoroughly. Spread onto warm crusty bread. Can also be used as a dip by adding a little water to make a dipping consistency.

LIBYAN POTATO PASTRIES (MAKES 12)

6oz/175g filo pastry

sunflower oil

1lb/450g potatoes, peeled

1 small onion, peeled and finely chopped

1 garlic clove, crushed

1 dessertspoon capers, chopped

2 tablespoons finely chopped fresh parsley

1 dessertspoon olive oil

black pepper

Cut the potatoes into even-sized chunks and boil them. Drain and mash, then add the onion, garlic, capers, parsley and olive oil. Season with black pepper, mix well and allow to cool.

Cut the filo pastry into 12 sheets of about 10 x 5 inches/25 x 13cm. Place the sheets on a flat surface and divide the filling between them, putting it in the left hand corner of each sheet. Starting at the left-hand corner, fold the pastry and filling over to the right, then up and then over to the left, folding the edges in as you go, to enclose the filling and form small triangles. Shallow fry the pastries in hot sunflower oil for a few minutes on each side until golden. Drain on kitchen paper and serve warm.

HERBED OLIVES

8oz/225g green olives

3 tablespoons finely chopped fresh coriander

3 tablespoons finely chopped fresh parsley

1 tablespoon finely chopped preserved lemon

1 garlic clove, crushed

1 small red chilli, finely chopped (optional)

2 tablespoons olive oil

2 tablespoons lemon juice

black pepper

Mix the olive oil with the lemon juice and add to the olives together with the remaining ingredients. Combine well, then transfer to a serving bowl, cover and refrigerate for 24 hours before serving.

PITTAS STUFFED WITH AUBERGINE AND CHICKPEAS (SERVES 4)

4 pitta breads

12oz/350g aubergine, finely diced

4oz/100g cooked chickpeas

1oz/25g dried dates, finely chopped

1 onion, peeled and finely chopped

2 tablespoons olive oil

6 fl.oz/175ml vegetable stock or water

1 teaspoon ground coriander

½ teaspoon ground cumin

¼ teaspoon ground cinnamon

black pepper

shredded crisp lettuce

plain soya yoghurt

Fry the aubergine and onion in the oil for 10 minutes, stirring frequently to prevent sticking. Add the dates, stock, coriander, cumin and cinnamon and season with black pepper. Stir well and bring to the boil. Simmer for 10 minutes, then add the chickpeas and continue simmering for a further 2 minutes. Warm the pitta breads and split them open. Put some shredded lettuce in each pitta and divide the filling between them. Top with a little plain yoghurt to serve.

SPICY VEGETABLE KEBABS (SERVES 4)

1lb/450g prepared vegetables (e.g. courgette, peppers, onion, aubergine, button mushrooms), cut into even-sized pieces

marinade

1 dessertspoon harissa

1 tablespoon olive oil

1 teaspoon lemon juice

1 shallot, peeled and chopped

1 garlic clove, chopped

¼ teaspoon paprika

black pepper

Blend the marinade ingredients until smooth and add to the vegetables in a mixing bowl. Stir until well combined, then cover and keep in the fridge for 4 hours. Thread the vegetables onto 8 small square skewers and place under a hot grill, turning occasionally, until just done. Serve with a salad garnish.

MOROCCAN PIZZAS (SERVES 4)

dough

12oz/350g plain flour

1 rounded teaspoon easy-blend yeast

½ teaspoon salt

2 tablespoons olive oil

approx. 6 fl.oz/175ml warm water

extra olive oil

filling

4oz/100g red pepper, finely chopped

4oz/100g tomato, skinned and chopped

2oz/50g mushrooms, wiped and chopped

1 onion, peeled and finely chopped

2 garlic cloves, crushed

6 black olives chopped

1oz/25g vegan 'cheese', grated

1 tablespoon olive oil

1 teaspoon ground cumin

½ teaspoon paprika

1 tablespoon finely chopped fresh parsley

black pepper

Mix the flour, yeast and salt in a large bowl. Stir in the 2 tablespoonfuls of oil, then gradually add the water until a soft dough forms. Knead the dough well and divide it into 4 equal portions.

Heat the oil for the filling and fry the red pepper, onion and garlic for 5 minutes. Remove from the heat and add the mushrooms, olives, 'cheese', cumin, paprika and parsley. Drain any juice from the tomato, then add the tomato to the mixture, season with black pepper and combine thoroughly.

Roll each piece of dough out into an 8 x 5 inch/20 x 13cm oblong. Divide the filling equally between the oblongs, spreading it out to within ½ inch/1cm of the edges. Fold one of the short sides of each oblong two-thirds of the way across and the other short side over the top, enclosing the filling, and press the edges together to join. Place the pizzas on a greased baking sheet and leave in a warm place for 1 hour to rise, then shallow fry them in hot olive oil for a few minutes on each side until golden brown. Drain on kitchen paper and serve warm.

SAVOURY ALMOND BALLS WITH TOMATO SAUCE (SERVES 4)

nut balls

2oz/50g ground almonds

2oz/50g natural minced textured vegetable protein

2oz/50g breadcrumbs

1 onion, peeled and finely chopped

1 garlic clove, crushed

1 dessertspoon olive oil

6 fl.oz/175ml vegetable stock

1 rounded tablespoon finely chopped fresh coriander

1 rounded teaspoon ground cumin

¼ teaspoon cayenne pepper

black pepper

extra olive oil

sauce

6oz/175g ripe tomatoes, skinned and chopped

1 small onion, peeled and finely chopped

½ small red chilli, finely chopped

1 tablespoon water

1 dessertspoon olive oil

1 dessertspoon tomato purée

½ teaspoon turmeric

½ teaspoon paprika

black pepper

finely chopped fresh coriander

Heat the dessertspoonful of oil for the nut balls and fry the onion and garlic until softened. Add the vegetable protein, stock, coriander, cumin and cayenne pepper and stir well. Season with black pepper, bring to the boil, cover and simmer for 5 minutes until the liquid has been absorbed. Remove from the heat and add the almonds and breadcrumbs, mixing thoroughly until everything binds together. Take rounded dessertspoonfuls of the mixture and roll into balls with damp hands. Put them on a plate, cover and refrigerate for a couple of hours.

Fry the onion and chilli in the oil for the sauce until soft. Add the tomatoes, tomato purée, turmeric, paprika and water and season with black pepper. Bring to the boil, then simmer gently for 5 minutes, stirring frequently, until the sauce thickens.

Either fry the nut balls in hot olive oil for a few minutes until browned and drain on kitchen paper, or alternatively brush them with olive oil, put them on a baking sheet and bake them in a preheated oven at 180°C/350°F/Gas mark 4 for about 20 minutes. Serve the nutballs with the reheated tomato sauce, garnished with fresh coriander.

SPINACH BUREEK (MAKES 8)

pastry
12oz/350g plain flour

1 rounded teaspoon easy-blend yeast

½ teaspoon salt

2 tablespoons olive oil

approx. 6 fl.oz/175ml warm water

extra olive oil

sesame seeds

filling
12oz/350g fresh spinach

2oz/50g vegan 'cheese', grated

1 onion, peeled and finely chopped

1 garlic clove, crushed

1 tablespoon olive oil

1 tablespoon finely chopped fresh dill

black pepper

Combine the flour, yeast and salt in a mixing bowl. Add the 2 tablespoonfuls of oil and stir well, then gradually add the water until a soft dough forms.

Knead the dough well, return it to the bowl, cover and leave to rise for an hour in a warm place.

Wash the spinach and put it in a large saucepan with only the water that clings to the leaves. Cook gently until tender, then drain and allow to cool. Squeeze out excess water and chop the spinach. Fry the onion and garlic in the oil until soft, remove from the heat and add the spinach, 'cheese' and dill. Season with black pepper and mix thoroughly.

Knead the dough again and divide it into 8 equal pieces. Roll each piece out on a floured board into a square of approximately 5 inches/13cm. Divide the filling between the squares, placing it on one diagonal half of each one only. Dampen the edges with water and fold the pastry over to make triangles, enclosing the filling. Press the edges together with a fork, then put the triangles on a greased baking sheet and leave in a warm place for 30 minutes. Brush the tops with olive oil and sprinkle with sesame seeds. Bake in a preheated oven at 180°C/350°F/Gas mark 4 for about 20 minutes until golden brown. Serve warm with a salad garnish.

SWEET POTATO AND GINGER PANCAKES (SERVES 4)

1lb/450g sweet potato, peeled
4 fl.oz/125ml soya milk
2oz/50g plain flour
1 teaspoon ground ginger
black pepper
sunflower oil

Cut the potato into even-sized chunks and boil for 10 minutes. Drain and allow to cool, then grate them into a bowl. Mix the flour and ginger with the soya milk until smooth, add to the potato, season with black pepper and combine well. Take rounded tablespoonfuls and put them in hot oil in a shallow pan. Flatten out each spoonful until about ¼inch/5mm thick and fry for a few minutes on each side until browned. Drain on kitchen paper and serve warm with a salad garnish.

SPICED AUBERGINE BRIOUATES (MAKES 12)

10oz/300g packet filo pastry

sunflower oil

ground cinnamon

filling

10oz/300g aubergine, finely chopped

2oz/50g prunes, stoned and finely chopped

1oz/25g natural minced textured vegetable protein

1 onion, peeled and finely chopped

1 garlic clove, crushed

2 tablespoons sunflower oil

1 rounded tablespoon finely chopped fresh coriander

6 fl.oz/175ml vegetable stock or water

½ teaspoon ground ginger

½ teaspoon paprika

½ teaspoon turmeric

½ teaspoon ground cumin

black pepper

Fry the aubergine, onion and garlic in the oil for 10 minutes. Add the rest of the filling ingredients and stir well, then bring to the boil, cover and simmer for 5 minutes. Uncover and simmer for 5 minutes more, stirring frequently, until the liquid has been absorbed. Remove from the heat and allow to cool. Cut the filo pastry into 24 sheets each of about 10 x 5 inches/25 x 13cm. Lay 12 sheets out on a flat surface and place another sheet on top of each one. Divide the filling between the 12 oblongs, putting it at one end only. Fold the two long sides over to enclose the edges of the filling, then roll each oblong up so that the filling is completely enclosed. Shallow fry the pastries in hot sunflower oil, turning until they are golden all over. Drain on kitchen paper and serve warm, lightly sprinkled with ground cinnamon.

Fava bean hummous (SERVES 4)

8oz/225g cooked fava beans

1 garlic clove, crushed

1 rounded tablespoon light tahini

1 tablespoon olive oil

1 tablespoon lemon juice

1 tablespoon water

½ teaspoon ground cumin

¼ teaspoon cayenne pepper

black pepper

Slip the skins from the beans, then mash them in a mixing bowl. Add the remaining ingredients and mix very well. Spoon into a serving bowl and serve with warm crusty bread.

SOUPS

Easily prepared and made from wholesome and nutritious ingredients, soups are occasionally served as starters, but are more usually treated as snacks throughout the day, or served as supper dishes or even for breakfast.

Harira, the national soup of Morocco, is traditionally eaten at dusk by Muslims during the holy month of Ramadan, to end each day of fasting. There are many regional variations of this soup, but most contain a hearty mix of vegetables and pulses combined with aromatic spices. In fact, it is often said that the air is filled with the aroma of harira during this fasting period.

Lentils, an important staple food in Egypt, are an especially popular soup ingredient there, while in Libya many soups are made with pasta.

HARIRA (SERVES 4)

8oz/225g cooked mixed beans

14oz/400g tin chopped tomatoes

4oz/100g red pepper, chopped

2oz/50g red lentils

2oz/50g long grain rice

1 onion, peeled and chopped

18 fl.oz/550ml vegetable stock

1 tablespoon olive oil

1 tablespoon lemon juice

2 tablespoons finely chopped fresh coriander

½ teaspoon turmeric

½ teaspoon ground ginger

½ teaspoon paprika

¼ teaspoon ground cinnamon

black pepper

fresh coriander leaves

Heat the oil in a large pan and fry the onion and red pepper for 5 minutes. Add the lentils, rice, stock, lemon juice, chopped coriander, turmeric, ginger, paprika and cinnamon and season with black pepper. Stir well and bring to the boil, then cover and simmer for 10 minutes, stirring occasionally. Add the tomatoes and mixed beans and continue simmering, covered, for another 20 minutes, again stirring occasionally to prevent sticking. Ladle the soup into serving bowls and garnish with fresh coriander leaves.

EGYPTIAN LENTIL SOUP (SERVES 4)

4oz/100g red lentils

4oz/100g ripe tomato, skinned and chopped

1 large onion, peeled and chopped

1 garlic clove, crushed

1 tablespoon olive oil

1 tablespoon lemon juice

1 rounded teaspoon ground cumin

½ teaspoon paprika

black pepper

22 fl.oz/650ml vegetable stock

finely chopped fresh coriander

Fry the onion and garlic in the oil in a large pan for 5 minutes. Add the tomato, lemon juice, cumin and paprika and cook until the tomato is soft, then add the lentils and stock and season with black pepper. Stir well and bring to the boil. Cover and simmer, stirring occasionally, for about 25 minutes until the lentils are cooked. Leave to cool slightly, then blend smooth. Serve at room temperature, garnished with chopped coriander.

PUMPKIN AND ORANGE SOUP (SERVES 4)

1¼lb/550g pumpkin flesh, chopped

1 onion, peeled and finely chopped

1 garlic clove, crushed

1 tablespoon olive oil

12 fl.oz/350ml fresh orange juice

8 fl.oz/225ml soya milk

½ teaspoon ground cumin

½ teaspoon ground coriander

½ teaspoon paprika

pinch of ground cinnamon

black pepper

finely chopped fresh parsley

Soften the onion and garlic in the oil in a large pan. Add the remaining ingredients apart from the soya milk and parsley and stir well. Bring to the boil, cover and simmer for about 15 minutes until the pumpkin is tender.

Allow to cool slightly, then blend until smooth. Pour the soup back into the cleaned pan, add the soya milk and reheat while stirring. Ladle the soup into bowls and garnish with chopped parsley.

CHILLED MINTED CUCUMBER SOUP (SERVES 4)

8oz/225g cucumber, chopped

4 rounded tablespoons chopped fresh mint

1 garlic clove, chopped

8 rounded tablespoons plain soya yoghurt

12 fl.oz/350ml cold vegetable stock

black pepper

fresh mint leaves

Put the cucumber, chopped mint, garlic, yoghurt and vegetable stock in a blender and season with black pepper. Blend smooth, then refrigerate until cold. Serve each bowl of soup garnished with fresh mint leaves.

SWEET POTATO AND GINGER SOUP (SERVES 4)

1lb/450g sweet potato, peeled and finely diced

1 inch/2.5cm piece of root ginger, peeled and finely chopped

4oz/100g tomato, skinned and chopped

1 onion, peeled and finely chopped

1 dessertspoon olive oil

18 fl.oz/550ml vegetable stock

½ teaspoon ground coriander

½ teaspoon paprika

¼ teaspoon cayenne pepper

black pepper

chopped fresh coriander

Heat the oil in a large pan and fry the onion and ginger for 5 minutes. Add the spices and tomato and cook until pulpy. Stir in the stock and potato and bring to the boil, cover and simmer for about 20 minutes until cooked. Allow to cool slightly, then transfer half of the mixture to a blender and blend until smooth. Return to the soup in the pan, stir well and reheat gently, then ladle the soup into bowls and garnish with fresh coriander.

CHICKPEA AND LENTIL SOUP (SERVES 4)

6oz/175g cooked chickpeas

4oz/100g red lentils

14oz/400g tin crushed tomatoes

1 onion, peeled and chopped

1 stick of celery, trimmed and finely sliced

1 garlic clove, crushed

½ inch/1cm piece of fresh ginger, peeled and finely chopped

1 tablespoon olive oil

1 tablespoon finely chopped fresh coriander

1 teaspoon ground cumin

½ teaspoon turmeric

¼ teaspoon ground cinnamon

black pepper

12 fl.oz/350ml vegetable stock

1 dessertspoon lemon juice

chopped fresh parsley

Fry the onion, celery, garlic and ginger in the oil for 5 minutes in a large pan. Add the spices, lentils and stock and stir well. Bring to the boil, cover and simmer gently, stirring occasionally, for 20 minutes. Add the tomatoes, chickpeas, coriander and lemon juice and combine well. Bring back to the boil, then cover and simmer for 5 minutes more, stirring occasionally. Garnish each bowl of soup with chopped parsley.

VEGETABLE AND VERMICELLI SOUP (SERVES 4)

6oz/175g leek, trimmed and sliced

6oz/175g ripe tomatoes, skinned and chopped

4oz/100g carrot, scraped and diced

4oz/100g turnip, peeled and diced

4oz/100g potato, peeled and diced

1 celery stick, trimmed and finely sliced

1 red onion, peeled and sliced

2oz/50g vermicelli

1 dessertspoon olive oil

few strands of saffron

28 fl.oz/825ml vegetable stock

black pepper

**   *garnish***

1 tablespoon finely chopped fresh coriander

1 tablespoon finely chopped fresh parsley

1 garlic clove, crushed

1 dessertspoon olive oil

1 teaspoon lemon juice

¼ teaspoon paprika

Heat the oil for the soup in a large pan and fry the leek, onion and celery for 5 minutes. Dissolve the saffron in the vegetable stock and add to the pan, together with the tomatoes, carrot, turnip and potato. Season with black pepper and stir well. Bring to the boil, cover and simmer for 10 minutes, then add the vermicelli and continue simmering for 15 minutes until done. Mix the garnish ingredients together and stir into the soup before serving.

SPINACH SOUP (SERVES 4)

2lb/900g fresh spinach leaves, shredded

1 onion, peeled and finely chopped

1 dessertspoon olive oil

20 fl.oz/600ml vegetable stock

black pepper

2 garlic cloves, crushed

2 dessertspoons olive oil

1 dessertspoon lemon juice

2 teaspoons ground coriander

¼ teaspoon cayenne pepper

plain soya yoghurt

Mix the garlic, 2 dessertspoonfuls of olive oil, lemon juice, ground coriander and cayenne pepper. Heat the remaining oil in a large pan and fry the onion for 5 minutes, then add the spinach and stock and season with black pepper. Bring to the boil, cover and simmer, stirring occasionally, for about 10 minutes until the spinach is tender. Transfer half of the soup to a blender and blend until smooth. Pour back into the rest of the soup and reheat, then add the garlic mixture. Stir well, ladle the soup into serving bowls and garnish with a swirl of yoghurt.

MINTED ROOT VEGETABLE AND BEAN SOUP (SERVES 4)

4oz/100g carrot, scraped and diced

4oz/100g sweet potato, peeled and diced

4oz/100g potato, peeled and diced

4oz/100g turnip, peeled and diced

6oz/175g cooked mixed beans

7oz/200g tin chopped tomatoes

14 fl.oz/425ml vegetable stock

1 onion, peeled and sliced

1 garlic clove, crushed

½ red chilli, finely chopped

1 dessertspoon olive oil

½ teaspoon paprika

½ teaspoon cumin seeds

black pepper

garnish

1 rounded teaspoon dried mint, crumbled

1 dessertspoon olive oil

1 teaspoon lemon juice

fresh mint leaves

Fry the onion, garlic and chilli in the oil for 5 minutes, add the vegetables, tomatoes, stock, paprika and cumin seeds and season with black pepper. Stir well, bring to the boil, then cover and simmer for about 20 minutes until tender. Pour a third of the mixture into a blender and blend smooth. Return to the soup in the pan and add the beans. Stir well, then simmer for 5 minutes, stirring regularly. Combine the dried mint with the oil and lemon juice, add to the soup and mix well. Garnish the bowls of soup with fresh mint leaves.

BUTTERNUT SQUASH AND PASTA SOUP (SERVES 4)

1lb/450g butternut squash, peeled and diced

4oz/100g tomato, skinned and chopped

1 onion, peeled and finely chopped

1 celery stick, trimmed and finely sliced

1 garlic clove, crushed

1 tablespoon olive oil

2oz/50g small pasta shapes

22 fl.oz/650ml vegetable stock

1 teaspoon cumin seeds

1 rounded teaspoon ground coriander

½ teaspoon paprika

black pepper

chopped fresh coriander

Soften the onion, celery and garlic in the oil. Add the tomatoes, cumin seeds, ground coriander and paprika and cook gently until pulpy, then stir in the vegetable stock and squash and season with black pepper. Bring to the boil, cover and simmer for 10 minutes. Blend half of the soup smooth, return it to the pan and add the pasta. Stir well and simmer for about 5 minutes until the pasta is done. Garnish each bowl of soup with chopped coriander.

GARLIC AND CHICKPEA SOUP (SERVES 4)

1lb/450g cooked chickpeas

1 onion, peeled and finely chopped

4 garlic cloves, crushed

1 small red chilli, finely chopped

1 tablespoon olive oil

20 fl.oz/600ml vegetable stock

2 rounded tablespoons finely chopped fresh coriander

black pepper

1 tablespoon lemon juice

extra chopped coriander

Fry the onion, garlic and chilli in the oil for 5 minutes. Add the chickpeas, vegetable stock and coriander and season with black pepper. Stir well and bring to the boil, then cover and simmer for 10 minutes. Pour half of the mixture into a blender and blend until smooth. Return to the soup in the pan and stir in the lemon juice. Garnish with chopped coriander when serving.

MAIN COURSES

Fragrantly spiced stews and tagines served on a bed of couscous are typical of the main courses to be found all over the region. Tagine is a word used in several of the countries and it refers to the earthenware, conically-lidded pot in which the stew is either cooked or served. In Libya stews served on a bed of pasta, especially macaroni, are equally popular and in Egypt rice is the more common accompaniment, although macaroni is often substituted for rice in kosheri, the Egyptian national dish. In Morocco seven is considered a magical number and dishes prepared with seven different vegetables are often served.

In many North African households the main meal of the day is eaten communally and with long-established ceremony. The cooked dishes are arranged on low tables and the diners first remove their shoes, then carefully wash their hands and sprinkle them with flower water. The host then breaks the bread and either this or the thumb and forefingers are used to scoop up the food.

SWEET POTATO-TOPPED TAGINE (SERVES 4)

1½lb/675g sweet potatoes, peeled and thinly sliced

8oz/225g carrot, scraped and chopped

4oz/100g parsnip, peeled and chopped

4oz/100g turnip, peeled and chopped

4oz/100g red pepper, sliced

4oz/100g green pepper, sliced

4oz/100g dried apricots, chopped

2oz/50g natural minced textured vegetable protein

1 onion, peeled and sliced

1 red chilli, finely chopped

2 garlic cloves, crushed

1 tablespoon olive oil

20 fl.oz/600ml vegetable stock

2 teaspoons ground cumin

1 rounded teaspoon ground ginger

½ teaspoon turmeric

black pepper

extra olive oil

toasted flaked almonds

Fry the onion, chilli and garlic in the tablespoonful of oil for 5 minutes in a large pan. Add the carrot, parsnip, turnip, red and green peppers, apricots, vegetable protein, stock and spices and stir well. Bring to the boil, cover and simmer, stirring occasionally, for 15 minutes, then spoon into a shallow ovenproof dish.

Boil the potato slices for 3 minutes, drain and arrange them on top of the vegetables. Brush the slices with olive oil and bake in a preheated oven at 180°C/350°F/Gas mark 4 for 30 minutes. Garnish with toasted flaked almonds and serve with a salad.

TUNISIAN VEGETABLE STEW (SERVES 4)

12oz/350g green cabbage

8oz/225g red pepper, sliced

8oz/225g yellow pepper, sliced

1 large onion, peeled and sliced

1 red chilli, finely chopped

8oz/225g cooked chickpeas

14oz/400g tin chopped tomatoes

1oz/25g raisins

2 tablespoons olive oil

1 tablespoon lemon juice

½ teaspoon turmeric

¼ teaspoon ground cinnamon

2 teaspoons ground coriander

black pepper

5 fl.oz/150ml vegetable stock or water

toasted pine kernels

Heat the oil in a large pan and fry the onion, chilli and red and yellow peppers for 5 minutes. Cut the thick stalks from the cabbage, finely shred the rest of the leaves and add to the pan. Fry for 5 minutes, stirring frequently, then add the remaining ingredients except the chickpeas and pine kernels and stir well. Bring to the boil, cover and simmer for 10 minutes, stirring occasionally. Add the chickpeas and continue simmering for 5 minutes more. Garnish with toasted pine kernels and serve on a bed of couscous or rice.

EGYPTIAN KOSHERI (SERVES 4)

12oz/350g long grain brown or white rice

lentil layer

8oz/225g red lentils

1 onion, peeled and finely chopped

1 garlic clove, crushed

1 dessertspoon olive oil

20 fl.oz/600ml vegetable stock

pinch of cayenne pepper

black pepper

sauce

14oz/400g tin chopped tomatoes

1 onion, peeled and finely chopped

2 garlic cloves, crushed

1 dessertspoon olive oil

1 dessertspoon red wine vinegar

1 teaspoon ground cumin

½ teaspoon paprika

black pepper

topping

1 onion, peeled and thinly sliced

1 dessertspoon olive oil

finely chopped fresh coriander

Heat the oil for the sauce and fry the onion and garlic for 5 minutes, add the remaining sauce ingredients and bring to the boil. Cover and simmer gently for 15 minutes, then remove from the heat.

Fry the onion and garlic in the oil for the lentil layer until softened. Add the lentils, stock and cayenne pepper and season with black pepper, stir well and bring to the boil. Cover and simmer, stirring occasionally, for about 20 minutes until the lentils are tender. Meanwhile cook the rice and fry the sliced onion in the oil until golden.

To assemble the dish, put the rice in a warmed serving dish and spoon the cooked lentils on top. Pour the reheated sauce over the lentils and top with the sliced onions and the fresh coriander. Serve with a salad and warm bread.

MOROCCAN VEGETABLE PAELLA (SERVES 4)

1½lb/675g prepared vegetables, diced (e.g. courgette, peppers, mushrooms, peas, green beans, carrot)

8oz/225g long grain rice

1 onion, peeled and finely chopped

2 garlic cloves, crushed

1 red chilli, finely chopped

1 tablespoon olive oil

2 tablespoons finely chopped fresh coriander

1 tablespoon tomato purée

1 tablespoon lemon juice

1 rounded teaspoon ground cumin

1 teaspoon paprika

½ teaspoon turmeric

black pepper

30 fl.oz/900ml vegetable stock

lemon wedges

black olives, halved

cherry tomatoes, halved

finely chopped fresh parsley

Heat the oil in a large pan and fry the onion, garlic and chilli until softened. Add the diced vegetables, rice, coriander, tomato purée, lemon juice, cumin, paprika, turmeric and stock and season with black pepper. Stir well and bring to the boil, then cover and simmer gently, stirring occasionally, until the liquid has been absorbed. Serve on warmed plates, garnished with lemon wedges, olives, tomatoes and parsley, with a green salad and warm bread.

BAKED SPINACH PANCAKES WITH TOMATO SAUCE (SERVES 4)

pancakes

3oz/75g plain flour

1oz/25g soya flour

5 fl.oz/150ml soya milk

5 fl.oz/150ml water

1 tablespoon olive oil

vegan margarine

filling

1lb/450g fresh spinach

4oz/100g leek, trimmed and finely sliced

½oz/15g raisins

1 garlic clove, crushed

1 dessertspoon olive oil

1 tablespoon finely chopped fresh dill

black pepper

sauce

8oz/225g ripe tomatoes, skinned and chopped

4 spring onions, trimmed and finely sliced

1 garlic clove, crushed

½ red chilli, finely chopped

1 dessertspoon olive oil

1 dessertspoon tomato purée

1 teaspoon lemon juice

1 tablespoon water

1 rounded tablespoon finely chopped fresh coriander

¼ teaspoon paprika

black pepper

Mix the plain with the soya flour in a large bowl. Add the soya milk, water and olive oil and whisk until smooth, then cover and leave for 1 hour. Whisk the batter again and heat a little margarine in a 7 inch/18cm non-stick frying pan until hot. Make 8 pancakes, using about 2 tablespoonfuls of batter for each one.

Wash the spinach and put it in a pan with only the water that clings to the leaves. Cook gently until tender, drain and allow to cool, then squeeze out any liquid and chop the spinach finely. Fry the leek and garlic in the oil until soft, add the spinach, raisins and dill and season with black pepper. Mix thoroughly, then divide the filling equally between the pancakes. Roll each pancake up to enclose the filling and pack them tightly in a greased baking dish. Bake in a preheated oven at 180°C/350°F/Gas mark 4 for 15 minutes.

Meanwhile, fry the spring onions, garlic and chilli in the oil for the sauce, add the remaining sauce ingredients and bring to the boil. Cover and simmer, stirring occasionally, until the tomatoes are soft and the sauce thickens. Mash the tomatoes with the back of a spoon to help break them up. Spoon the sauce over the pancakes and serve with a grain dish and salad.

MEDITERRANEAN TAGINE (SERVES 4)

12oz/350g courgette, chopped

8oz/225g carrot, scraped and finely chopped

8oz/225g cooked haricot beans

4oz/100g green pepper, chopped

4oz/100g red pepper, chopped

4oz/100g mushrooms, wiped and sliced

½oz/15g sun-dried tomatoes

14oz/400g tin chopped tomatoes

1 red onion, peeled and sliced

2 garlic cloves, crushed

6 fl.oz/175ml vegetable stock or water

1 tablespoon lemon juice

1 tablespoon olive oil

2 tablespoons finely chopped fresh parsley

1 teaspoon cumin seeds

1 rounded dessertspoon harissa

black pepper

chopped olives

Soak the sun-dried tomatoes in the stock for 1 hour. Fry the onion, garlic and carrot in the oil for 5 minutes, then add the soaked tomatoes and stock together with the remaining ingredients apart from the beans and olives. Stir well and bring to the boil. Cover and simmer for 10 minutes, stirring regularly. Add the beans and continue simmering for 5-10 minutes, stirring frequently, until the vegetables are done. Transfer to a warmed serving dish and garnish with chopped olives. Serve with couscous or a grain dish and bread.

SEVEN VEGETABLE TAGINE (SERVES 4)

8oz/225g French beans, topped, tailed and cut into 1 inch/2.5cm lengths

8oz/225g courgette, diced

8oz/225g tomatoes, skinned and chopped

6oz/175g carrot, scraped and diced

6oz/175g turnip, peeled and diced

6oz/175g butternut squash, peeled and diced

1 onion, peeled and chopped

1 green chilli, finely chopped

2 garlic cloves, crushed

12 fl.oz/350ml vegetable stock

1 tablespoon olive oil

3 tablespoons finely chopped fresh coriander

1 rounded teaspoon cumin seeds

1 teaspoon ground ginger

1 teaspoon turmeric

1 teaspoon paprika

black pepper

finely chopped fresh parsley

Fry the onion, chilli and garlic for 5 minutes in the oil in a large pan. Add the cumin seeds, ginger, turmeric and paprika and stir around for a few seconds, then the tomatoes, carrot, turnip, squash and stock and stir well. Season with black pepper and bring to the boil, cover and simmer, stirring occasionally, for 20 minutes. Add the courgette, French beans and coriander, bring back to the boil, cover and simmer for another 20 minutes, stirring frequently, until cooked. Spoon into a warmed dish, garnish with parsley and serve with couscous or a grain dish and bread.

RUSTIC MEDITERRANEAN PIE (SERVES 4)

pastry

4oz/100g plain wholemeal flour

4oz/100g plain flour

4oz/100g vegan margarine

cold water

filling

6oz/175g tomatoes, skinned and chopped

4oz/100g courgette, chopped

4oz/100g red pepper, chopped

4oz/100g yellow pepper, chopped

4oz/100g aubergine, diced

4oz/100g cooked mixed beans

2oz/50g mushrooms, wiped and chopped

1oz/25g black olives, chopped

1 red onion, peeled and finely chopped

2 garlic cloves, crushed

1 tablespoon olive oil

1 tablespoon water

1 dessertspoon tomato purée

1 rounded tablespoon finely chopped fresh oregano

1 rounded tablespoon finely chopped fresh marjoram

½ teaspoon paprika

black pepper

pine kernels

fresh oregano and marjoram leaves

Heat the oil in a large pan and fry the aubergine, onion and garlic until softened. Add the tomatoes, courgette, red and yellow peppers, mushrooms, tomato purée, water, chopped oregano and marjoram and paprika, season with black pepper and stir well. Cook the mixture for 10 minutes, stirring regularly, until softened. Remove from the heat and stir in the cooked beans and olives.

Mix the two flours in a large bowl, rub in the margarine and add enough cold water to bind. Turn the pastry out onto a floured board and knead well, then roll it out into a circle of about 12 inches/30cm. Put this on a greased baking sheet and pile the filling in the middle. Fold the edges of the pastry in to partly enclose the filling, leaving the centre open. Sprinkle the open filling with pine kernels and bake the pie in a preheated oven at 180°C/350°F/Gas mark 4 for about 30 minutes until golden brown. Garnish with oregano and marjoram leaves and serve with salad or vegetable accompaniments.

AUBERGINE, COURGETTE AND CHICKPEA TAGINE (SERVES 4)

12oz/350g aubergine, diced

8oz/225g courgette, chopped

8oz/225g cooked chickpeas

14oz/400g tin chopped tomatoes

1oz/25g natural minced textured vegetable protein

1 red onion, peeled and chopped

2 garlic cloves, crushed

6 fl.oz/175ml vegetable stock or water

3 tablespoons olive oil

1 tablespoon lemon juice

1 dessertspoon tomato purée

1 rounded dessertspoon harissa

1 rounded teaspoon ground coriander

½ teaspoon paprika

¼ teaspoon ground cinnamon

black pepper

toasted flaked almonds

Fry the aubergine, onion and garlic in the oil, stirring frequently, for 10 minutes. Add the remaining ingredients except the chickpeas and almonds and stir well. Bring to the boil, cover and simmer for 5 minutes. Remove from the heat and stir in the chickpeas, then transfer to a shallow ovenproof dish and cover with foil. Bake in a preheated oven at 180°C/350°F/Gas mark 4 for 30 minutes. Serve garnished with toasted flaked almonds, with couscous and a green salad.

ROOT VEGETABLE AND LENTIL STEW (SERVES 4)

12oz/350g potato, scraped and diced

10oz/300g carrot, scraped and diced

8oz/225g turnip, peeled and diced

6oz/175g red lentils

4oz/100g prunes, stoned and chopped

1 onion, peeled and finely chopped

1 tablespoon olive oil

1 rounded teaspoon ground ginger

1 teaspoon turmeric

1 teaspoon paprika

¼ teaspoon ground cinnamon

black pepper

22 fl.oz/650ml vegetable stock

toasted flaked almonds

Fry the onion for 5 minutes in the oil in a large pan. Add the spices and stir around for 30 seconds, then put in the diced vegetables, lentils, prunes and stock and stir well. Bring to the boil, cover and simmer gently, stirring frequently, for about 25 minutes until everything is done and the mixture is thick. Serve on a bed of couscous or a grain, garnished with toasted almonds and accompanied by bread and salad.

RATATOUILLE-STUFFED PITTAS (SERVES 4)

4 pitta breads
chopped black olives
finely chopped fresh parsley
filling
1lb/450g aubergine, diced
12oz/350g courgette, sliced
8oz/225g tomatoes, skinned and cut into wedges
4oz/100g red pepper, sliced
4oz/100g yellow pepper, sliced
4oz/100g mushrooms, wiped and sliced
4oz/100g cooked chickpeas
1 red onion, peeled and sliced
4 garlic cloves, crushed
4 tablespoons olive oil
1 rounded tablespoon finely chopped fresh marjoram
1 rounded tablespoon finely chopped fresh oregano
black pepper

Heat the oil in a large pan and fry the aubergine, red and yellow peppers, onion and garlic for 15 minutes, stirring frequently to prevent sticking. Add the courgette, marjoram and oregano and season with black pepper. Continue cooking for 5 minutes, then add the tomatoes, mushrooms and chickpeas and cook for another 5 minutes or so until the mixture is thick and the vegetables are tender. Warm the pitta breads and split them open. Fill each pitta with some of the filling and garnish with chopped olives and parsley. Serve with a grain dish and a green salad.

GREEN VEGETABLE, TOMATO AND CHICKPEA STEW (SERVES 4)

12oz/350g courgette, sliced

8oz/225g French beans, topped, tailed and cut into 1 inch/2.5cm
lengths

8oz/225g green pepper, chopped

8oz/225g fresh spinach, shredded

14oz/400g tin crushed tomatoes

8oz/225g cooked chickpeas

½oz/15g raisins

1 onion, peeled and chopped

1 green chilli, finely chopped

2 garlic cloves, crushed

1 tablespoon olive oil

1 rounded tablespoon finely chopped fresh dill

1 rounded tablespoon finely chopped fresh coriander

¼ teaspoon grated nutmeg

black pepper

chopped walnuts

Fry the onion, chilli and garlic in the oil in a large pan for 5 minutes. Add the spinach and cook until it wilts, then stir in the tomatoes, courgette, French beans, green pepper, raisins, dill, coriander and nutmeg. Season with black pepper and simmer for 15 minutes. Add the chickpeas and continue simmering, stirring occasionally, until the vegetables are cooked, adding a little water if necessary to prevent sticking. Garnish with chopped walnuts and serve with a grain dish and bread and salad accompaniments.

APRICOT AND SQUASH STEW (SERVES 4)

1½lb/675g butternut squash, peeled and diced

12oz/350g courgette, chopped

8oz/225g fresh apricots, stoned and diced

1 onion, peeled and finely chopped

2 garlic cloves, crushed

1oz/25g dried dates, finely chopped

1 tablespoon olive oil

12 fl.oz/350ml vegetable stock

2 tablespoons finely chopped fresh coriander

2 teaspoons ground coriander

1 teaspoon ground ginger

½ teaspoon turmeric

½ teaspoon nutmeg

black pepper

toasted flaked almonds

Soften the onion and garlic in the oil for 5 minutes. Add the ground coriander, ginger, turmeric and nutmeg and stir around for 30 seconds. Add the butternut squash, courgette, apricots, dates, fresh coriander and stock and season with black pepper, stir well and bring to the boil. Cover and simmer for about 20 minutes, stirring occasionally, until done. Serve garnished with flaked almonds, with a grain dish and bread.

COUSCOUS AND GRAIN ACCOMPANIMENTS

Primitive couscous pots have been unearthed in ancient tombs, dating the eating of couscous back to the days when the nomadic Berber tribes roamed across the region around 4,000 years ago. Today couscous is still a fundamental and staple food in many parts of North Africa. It is prepared in a special pot called a couscousière – a type of double pan in which the couscous is steamed in the top part over the stew which is simmering in the bottom. The stew is then served on a bed of couscous, which can be plain, flavoured with herbs or spices or mixed with a multitude of other ingredients.

Rice, one of the main crops grown in the Nile valley, is the most important grain eaten in Egypt and it is served either plainly cooked or spiced and mixed with other ingredients. Other popular grains include wheat, barley and millet and these too are served either plain or flavoured with herbs or spices.

Couscous (SERVES 4)

8oz/225g couscous
16 fl.oz/475ml hot water or vegetable stock
¼ teaspoon turmeric (optional)

Dissolve the turmeric in the hot water or vegetable stock and add the couscous. Leave to soak for 5 minutes until the liquid has been absorbed. Transfer to a fine sieve and fluff up the grains to separate them, then put the sieve over a pan of simmering water or stew. Cover and steam for 10 minutes.

Couscous with sweetcorn (SERVES 4)

As above, but add 8oz/225g cooked sweetcorn kernels to the cooked couscous.

Couscous with peas (SERVES 4)

Cook the couscous as above and add 8oz/225g cooked peas before serving.

Couscous with pine kernels (SERVES 4)

Stir 1oz/25g toasted pine kernels into the cooked couscous.

Minted couscous (SERVES 4)

Add 1 rounded dessertspoon crumbled dried mint to the water or vegetable stock in which the couscous is to be soaked, then follow the recipe above.

SAFFRON COUSCOUS WITH SWEET PEPPERS (SERVES 4)

8oz/225g couscous

8oz/225g mixed peppers, finely chopped

1 tablespoon olive oil

few strands of saffron

black pepper

16 fl.oz/475ml hot vegetable stock

Fry the peppers in the oil until soft. Dissolve the saffron in the hot vegetable stock and add, together with the couscous. Season with black pepper and stir well, then remove from the heat, cover and leave for 15 minutes. Stir well to fluff up before serving.

MUSHROOM AND CORIANDER COUSCOUS (SERVES 4)

8oz/225g couscous

6oz/175g mushrooms, wiped and finely chopped

1 garlic clove, crushed

1 tablespoon olive oil

2 rounded tablespoons finely chopped fresh coriander

black pepper

16 fl.oz/475ml hot vegetable stock

Heat the oil in a pan and fry the mushrooms and garlic until the juices run. Remove from the heat and add the remaining ingredients. Stir well, cover and allow to stand for 15 minutes. Fluff up by stirring.

SPICY FRUIT AND NUT COUSCOUS (SERVES 4)

8oz/225g couscous

4oz/100g dried apricots, finely chopped

1oz/25g sultanas

1oz/25g mixed nuts, chopped

1 onion, peeled and finely chopped

1 tablespoon olive oil

10 fl.oz/300ml fresh orange juice

10 fl.oz/300ml water

1 teaspoon coriander seeds, crushed

8 cloves

½ teaspoon turmeric

2 inch/5cm cinnamon stick, broken

black pepper

1 orange, peeled and cut into slices

Soften the onion in the oil. Add the apricots, sultanas, orange juice, water, coriander seeds, cloves, turmeric and cinnamon stick, season with black pepper and bring to the boil. Simmer for 1 minute, then remove from the heat and stir in the couscous. Cover and leave for 15 minutes. Stir in the nuts, spoon into a serving dish and garnish with the orange slices before serving.

HERBED BARLEY (SERVES 4)

8oz/225g pot barley

2 pints/1.2 litres boiling water

2 tablespoons olive oil

4 rounded tablespoons finely chopped fresh mixed herbs (e.g. parsley, oregano, mint)

1 onion, peeled and finely chopped

black pepper

Soak the barley in the boiling water in a large pan for 2 hours, then put the pan on the cooker and bring to the boil. Cover and simmer for about 40 minutes until the liquid has been absorbed and the barley is done. Towards the end of the cooking time fry the onion in the oil until soft. Add the cooked barley and the herbs, season with black pepper, stir around for a couple of minutes and serve.

EGYPTIAN RICE (SERVES 4)

8oz/225g long grain rice

4oz/100g button mushrooms, wiped and sliced

2oz/50g natural minced textured vegetable protein

1 onion, peeled and finely chopped

1 tablespoon olive oil

black pepper

30 fl.oz/900ml hot vegetable stock

1 teaspoon ground cumin

1oz/25g flaked almonds, toasted

plain soya yoghurt

Fry the onion in the oil for 5 minutes. Add the mushrooms and fry for 2 minutes more, then remove from the heat and add the vegetable protein, stock and ground cumin. Stir, cover and leave to soak for 10 minutes. Return to the heat, add the rice and season with black pepper, then bring to the boil, cover and simmer gently until the liquid has been absorbed. Stir in three quarters of the flaked almonds and spoon the rice into a warmed serving dish. Garnish with plain yoghurt and the remaining almonds.

SPICED MILLET WITH CARROTS (SERVES 4)

8oz/225g millet

8oz/225g carrot, scraped and finely chopped

1 onion, peeled and finely chopped

24 fl.oz/725ml vegetable stock

1 tablespoon olive oil

2 tablespoons finely chopped fresh coriander

½ teaspoon turmeric

1 teaspoon cumin seeds

black pepper

Heat the oil and fry the carrot and onion for 5 minutes. Add the millet, turmeric and cumin seeds and stir around for 30 seconds, then the stock and half of the coriander. Stir well, season with black pepper and bring to the boil. Cover and simmer gently until the liquid has been absorbed. Transfer to a serving dish and garnish with the remaining coriander.

RICE WITH SWISS CHARD AND WALNUTS (SERVES 4)

8oz/225g long grain rice

8oz/225g Swiss chard, finely shredded

1 onion, peeled and finely chopped

2 garlic cloves, crushed

2 tablespoons olive oil

20 fl.oz/600ml vegetable stock

1 tablespoon finely chopped fresh mint

1 tablespoon finely chopped fresh dill

black pepper

1oz/25g walnuts, finely chopped

Fry the Swiss chard, onion and garlic in the oil until soft. Add the rice, stock, mint and dill and season with black pepper. Stir well and bring to the boil, then cover and simmer gently until the liquid has been absorbed. Remove from the heat and stir in the walnuts before serving.

MINTED BULGAR WHEAT WITH GREEN VEGETABLES (SERVES 4)

8oz/225g bulgar wheat

8oz/225g shelled broad beans

4oz/100g green pepper, chopped

4oz/100g French beans, topped, tailed and cut into ½ inch/1cm lengths

4oz/100g shelled peas

1 onion, peeled and finely chopped

2 garlic cloves, crushed

1 small green chilli, finely chopped

20 fl.oz/600ml vegetable stock or water

2 tablespoons olive oil

2 rounded teaspoons dried mint

black pepper

chopped pistachios

fresh mint leaves

Steam the broad beans until just tender, then rinse under cold running water and carefully remove the skins. Heat the oil in a large pan and fry the green pepper, French beans, onion, garlic and chilli for 5 minutes. Add the broad beans, peas, bulgar wheat, vegetable stock and dried mint, season with black pepper and stir well. Bring to the boil, then cover and simmer very gently until the liquid has been absorbed. Spoon into a serving dish and garnish with chopped pistachios and fresh mint leaves.

SPICED FRUIT AND NUT RICE (SERVES 4)

8oz/225g long grain brown rice

2oz/50g dried apricots, finely chopped

1oz/25g sultanas

1 onion, peeled and finely chopped

1 tablespoon olive oil

1 inch/2.5cm cinnamon stick

1 teaspoon coriander seeds, crushed

½ teaspoon turmeric

½ teaspoon ground ginger

black pepper

5 fl.oz/150ml fresh orange juice

17 fl.oz/500ml water

11/2oz/40g mixed nuts, chopped

1 orange, peeled and sliced

Heat the oil in a pan and fry the onion for 5 minutes, then add the spices and rice and stir around for 30 seconds. Stir in the apricots, sultanas, orange juice and water and bring to the boil. Cover and simmer gently until the liquid has been absorbed. Mix in three quarters of the nuts and serve garnished with the orange slices and remaining nuts.

VEGETABLES

Vegetable dishes are very versatile and can be used as accompaniments to main courses or a selection of two or three served with a grain can form the main course itself. They are also often served as starters and as snacks throughout the day. Marinating and baking vegetables is an especially popular way of cooking them and the Moroccan marinades called charmoulas on page 92 are ideal for this purpose. For a quickly prepared dish with a North African flavour, serve plainly cooked vegetables with one of the sauces or dressings from page 90–93.

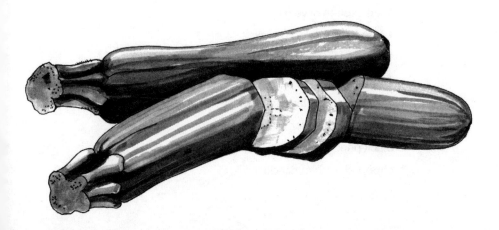

SPINACH WITH TOMATOES AND BEANS (SERVES 4)

1lb/450g fresh spinach

8oz/225g tomatoes, skinned and chopped

6oz/175g cooked blackeye beans

1 onion, peeled and chopped

1 garlic clove, crushed

1 tablespoon olive oil

½ teaspoon ground cumin

black pepper

cherry tomatoes

Fry the onion and garlic in the oil in a large saucepan for 3 minutes. Wash the spinach and squeeze out any excess liquid, then chop it and add to the pan. Cover and cook gently for about 5 minutes until wilted. Add the tomatoes and cumin and season with black pepper. Raise the heat and simmer uncovered, stirring occasionally, for 5 minutes. Add the beans and continue simmering for another 5 minutes. Transfer to a warmed serving dish and garnish with quartered cherry tomatoes.

SPICED SWEET POTATOES (SERVES 4)

1½lb/675g sweet potatoes, peeled and diced

1 onion, peeled and finely chopped

1 tablespoon olive oil

1 teaspoon ground ginger

1 teaspoon ground cumin

1 teaspoon paprika

1 dessertspoon lemon juice

6 fl.oz/175ml water

black pepper

chopped fresh coriander

Heat the oil in a large pan and fry the onion until softened. Add the ginger, cumin and paprika and stir around for 30 seconds, then the potato, lemon juice and water and season with black pepper. Stir well and bring to the boil. Cover and simmer, stirring occasionally, for about 20 minutes until cooked. Serve garnished with chopped coriander.

BAKED VEGETABLE CHARMOULA (SERVES 4)

4oz/100g courgette, halved lengthwise and sliced

4oz/100g red pepper, sliced

4oz/100g green pepper, sliced

4oz/100g tomato, cut into wedges

4oz/100g mushrooms, wiped and sliced

½ onion, peeled and sliced

chopped fresh parsley

charmoula

½ onion, peeled and chopped

1 garlic clove, chopped

¼ green chilli, chopped

½ teaspoon ground cumin

½ teaspoon paprika

1 tablespoon chopped fresh coriander

1 tablespoon olive oil

1 dessertspoon lemon juice

1 dessertspoon water

black pepper

Put the prepared vegetables apart from the parsley in a mixing bowl. Place the charmoula ingredients in a blender and blend until smooth, then add to the vegetables and mix well. Transfer everything to a baking dish, cover with foil and leave to marinate for 1 hour. Bake covered in a preheated oven at 180°C/350°F/Gas mark 4 for about 45 minutes until the vegetables are tender. Garnish with chopped fresh parsley to serve.

KALE WITH GARLIC AND DILL DRESSING (SERVES 4)

12oz/350g kale

2 tablespoons olive oil

1 dessertspoon lemon juice

2 tablespoons finely chopped fresh dill

1 garlic clove, crushed

black pepper

chopped walnuts

Cut the thick stalks from the kale and discard. Finely shred the leaves and steam until tender. Mix the oil with the lemon juice, dill and garlic and season with black pepper, add to the cooked kale and toss thoroughly. Transfer to a serving dish and garnish with chopped walnuts.

TUNISIAN SPICED CARROTS (SERVES 4)

1¼lb/550g carrots, scraped

1 garlic clove, crushed

1 rounded teaspoon coriander seeds

1 rounded teaspoon caraway seeds

2 tablespoons olive oil

2 tablespoons lemon juice

black pepper

chopped fresh coriander

Thinly slice the carrots lengthways and cut each slice into diagonal shapes. Dry roast the coriander and caraway seeds, then grind them in a mortar with a pestle.

Heat the oil and fry the carrots and garlic for 5 minutes. Add the spices and lemon juice and continue cooking, stirring regularly, until done. Serve with a garnish of fresh coriander.

ROASTED PEPPERS WITH COURGETTES (SERVES 4)

1lb/450g mixed peppers

1lb/450g courgette, chopped

4oz/100g tomato, skinned and chopped

2 garlic cloves

1 onion, peeled and chopped

1 tablespoon olive oil

2 tablespoons chopped fresh coriander

1 rounded teaspoon ground cumin

½ teaspoon paprika

black pepper

1 dessertspoon lemon juice

4 fl.oz/125ml water

chopped fresh parsley

Grill the peppers, turning them occasionally, until the skins blister. Allow to cool slightly, then carefully remove the skins, stalks, membranes and seeds and chop the flesh. Blend the onion and garlic with the oil, then transfer to a saucepan and cook gently for 10 minutes, stirring occasionally. Add the tomato, ground cumin, paprika and lemon juice and simmer until the tomato is pulpy. Stir in the courgette, coriander and water, season with black pepper and bring to the boil. Cook gently for 10 minutes, then add the chopped peppers and continue simmering for a few minutes more, stirring regularly, until tender. Spoon into a serving dish and garnish with chopped parsley.

MINTED POTATO AND 'CHEESE' CROQUETTES (SERVES 4)

2lb/900g potatoes, peeled

2oz/50g vegan 'cheese', grated

1oz/25g vegan margarine

1 rounded dessertspoon dried mint, crumbled

black pepper

2oz/50g breadcrumbs

olive oil

Cut the potatoes into even-sized chunks and boil them. Drain and dry them off over a low heat, then mash with the margarine. Stir in the grated 'cheese' and mint and season with black pepper. Mix well, cover and refrigerate until cold. Take rounded tablespoonfuls of the mixture and shape into croquettes. Roll each croquette in breadcrumbs until completely covered, put them on an oiled baking tray and brush them with olive oil. Bake in a preheated oven at 180°C/350°F/Gas mark 4 for 30 minutes until golden brown.

ROASTED AUBERGINE WITH RED ONION (SERVES 4)

1lb/450g aubergine

1 red onion, peeled and sliced

1 garlic clove, crushed

4 tablespoons olive oil

2 tablespoons lemon juice

2 tablespoons water

1 teaspoon paprika

1 teaspoon ground cumin

1 teaspoon ground coriander

black pepper

chopped fresh coriander

Slice the aubergine lengthways into ¼ inch/5mm thick slices. Quarter each slice and put them in a bowl with the red onion. Mix the olive oil with the lemon juice, water, paprika, cumin, coriander and garlic, add to the vegetables and season with black pepper. Stir thoroughly until the vegetables are coated. Transfer to a shallow baking dish and bake in a preheated oven at 180°C/350°F/Gas mark 4 for about 30 minutes, stirring occasionally, until tender. Garnish with chopped coriander when serving.

ALGERIAN GREEN BEANS WITH ALMONDS (SERVES 4)

12oz/350g French beans, topped, tailed and cut into 1 inch/2.5cm
   lengths

1oz/25g flaked almonds

2 tablespoons olive oil

1 garlic clove, crushed

1 teaspoon ground cumin

½ teaspoon paprika

black pepper

Steam the beans until just done. Meanwhile fry the almonds, garlic, cumin and paprika gently in the oil until the almonds are golden. Add the hot cooked beans, season with black pepper and toss thoroughly before serving.

SPICY CHICKPEAS WITH TOMATOES AND PEPPERS (SERVES 4)

8oz/225g cooked chickpeas

8oz/225g tomatoes, skinned and chopped

4oz/100g red pepper, chopped

4oz/100g green pepper, chopped

1 onion, peeled and finely chopped

1 garlic clove, crushed

1 tablespoon olive oil

1 rounded tablespoon finely chopped fresh coriander

1 dessertspoon lemon juice

1 rounded teaspoon harissa

1 teaspoon cumin seeds

½ teaspoon paprika

black pepper

chopped fresh parsley

Fry the red and green peppers, onion and garlic in the oil for 5 minutes. Add the tomatoes, lemon juice, harissa, cumin seeds, paprika and coriander. Season with black pepper and stir well, then simmer for 5 minutes, stirring occasionally. Add the chickpeas and continue simmering for a couple of minutes more. Serve garnished with chopped parsley.

BROAD BEANS WITH COURGETTES (SERVES 4)

12oz/350g shelled broad beans

12oz/350g courgette, chopped

1 onion, peeled and finely chopped

2 garlic cloves, crushed

1 tablespoon olive oil

4 tablespoons water

1 teaspoon dried mint

black pepper

1 tablespoon lemon juice

chopped fresh parsley

Steam the broad beans until just tender, drain and rinse under cold running water and slip the beans from their skins. Heat the oil and fry the onion and garlic for 5 minutes, then add the courgette, water and mint and season with black pepper. Bring to the boil, cover and simmer, stirring occasionally, for 5 minutes. Add the broad beans and continue cooking for a further 5 minutes. Remove from the heat and stir in the lemon juice. Spoon into a serving dish and garnish with chopped parsley.

BREADS

Breads form a very important part of the North African diet and some type of bread is served with every meal. Pittas are typically stuffed with savoury fillings and served as snacks, while plain pittas, French sticks and other breads are used to scoop up stews and couscous or to mop up soups. Stale bread is chopped and added to salads or made into breadcrumbs and used in sweet and savoury recipes. All home-made breads are best eaten on the day of baking, but they can be wrapped in foil and frozen.

ALGERIAN ANISE BREAD

12oz/350g plain wholemeal flour

½ sachet easy-blend yeast

½ teaspoon salt

1 tablespoon aniseeds

1 tablespoon demerara sugar

2 tablespoons sunflower oil

approx. 6 fl.oz/175ml warm water

extra sunflower oil

Mix the flour, yeast, salt, aniseeds and sugar in a large bowl, add the oil and combine well. Gradually add the water until a soft dough forms. Knead the dough, return it to the bowl, cover and leave in a warm place for 1 hour until risen. Knead the dough again, then divide it into 6 equal pieces. Roll each piece into a ball and arrange 5 of the balls in a circle on a greased baking sheet. Place the remaining ball in the centre and gently squeeze the dough together so that no gaps remain. Leave in a warm place for 30 minutes to rise, then brush the top with sunflower oil and bake in a preheated oven at 200°C/400°F/Gas mark 6 for about 20 minutes until golden brown. Allow to cool on a wire rack before serving.

SESAME BREAD RINGS (MAKES 8)

12oz/350g plain flour

1oz/25g sesame seeds

½ sachet easy-blend yeast

½ teaspoon salt

2 tablespoons sunflower oil

1 dessertspoon light tahini

approx. 7 fl.oz/200ml warm water

soya milk

extra sesame seeds

Put the flour, 1oz/25g sesame seeds, yeast and salt in a bowl, add the sunflower oil and mix well. Dissolve the tahini in the warm water and gradually add to the mixture until a soft dough forms. Knead the dough well and return it to the bowl. Cover and leave to rise for 45 minutes in a warm place, then knead the dough again. Divide it into 8 equal portions and roll each one into a ball in the palm of the hand, then make a hole in the centre of each ball with a thumb. Widen the openings slightly to form rings and put them on a greased baking sheet. Leave to rise again in a warm place for 45 minutes, then brush the rings with soya milk and sprinkle with sesame seeds. Bake in a preheated oven at 200°C/400°F/Gas mark 6 for about 15 minutes until golden. Slide onto a wire rack to cool.

CORIANDER AND ORANGE BREAD

8oz/225g plain flour

1 rounded teaspoon easy-blend yeast

½ teaspoon salt

1 tablespoon coriander seeds, crushed

2 tablespoons finely grated orange zest

1oz/25g vegan margarine, melted

approx. 4 fl.oz/125ml soya milk, warmed

extra soya milk

Combine the flour, salt, yeast, coriander seeds and orange zest in a bowl and mix in the melted margarine. Gradually add the soya milk until a soft dough forms. Knead the dough for 5 minutes, then shape it into a 6 inch/15cm circle and place it on a greased baking sheet. Leave in a warm place for 1 hour until risen. Brush the top with soya milk and mark a cross on top with a sharp knife. Bake in a preheated oven at 200°C/400°F/Gas mark 6 for 15-20 minutes until browned. Serve warm.

OLIVE FLAT BREAD

8oz/225g plain flour

½ sachet easy-blend yeast

½ teaspoon salt

1oz/25g black olives, chopped

2 tablespoons olive oil

approx. 4 fl.oz/125ml warm water

8 black olives, halved

extra olive oil

Put the flour, yeast and salt in a mixing bowl, add the chopped olives and olive oil and combine thoroughly, then gradually add the water until a soft dough forms. Knead the dough well and shape into a flat round of about 7 inches/18cm diameter. Transfer to a greased baking sheet and allow to rise for an hour in a warm place. Brush with olive oil and lightly score the top in a diamond pattern. Press an olive half into each diamond, then bake in a preheated oven at 200°C/400°F/Gas mark 6 for about 15 minutes until golden brown. Serve warm.

SALADS

Lightly spiced or Mediterranean-style herb-flavoured salads are popular throughout the region and are served as accompaniments to main courses and as snacks. Salads made from oranges and carrots are also particular favourites and variations are found in several of the countries. A multitude of salads are made from beans and lentils and these are particularly useful for filling pitta breads, to serve as light meals.

TUNISIAN AUBERGINE SALAD (SERVES 4)

12oz/350g aubergine, diced

6oz/175g red pepper

6oz/175g tomatoes, skinned and chopped

1 garlic clove, crushed

1 tablespoon olive oil

2 rounded tablespoons finely chopped fresh oregano

1 teaspoon red wine vinegar

black pepper

grated vegan 'cheese'

chopped fresh parsley

Grill the red pepper until the skin blisters, then carefully remove skin, stalk, membranes and seeds. Chop the flesh and put it in a mixing bowl with the drained chopped tomatoes. Steam the aubergine until tender and add to the bowl, together with the oregano. Mix the garlic with the oil and vinegar and pour over the salad, season with black pepper and mix thoroughly. Transfer to a serving bowl, cover and keep in the fridge until cold. Garnish with grated 'cheese' and chopped parsley before serving.

CARROT AND ORANGE SALAD (SERVES 4)

1lb/450g carrots, scraped and grated

2 oranges, peeled and sliced

1oz/25g dried dates, finely chopped

2 dessertspoons olive oil

2 dessertspoons fresh orange juice

½ teaspoon paprika

black pepper

½oz/15g pine kernels, toasted

Put the carrots in a bowl with the dates and pine kernels, mix the oil with the orange juice and paprika and add. Season with black pepper and combine well. Arrange the orange slices on a serving plate and pile the salad on top.

Spiced green lentil salad (serves 4)

4oz/100g green lentils

6oz/175g courgette, chopped

4oz/100g tomato, skinned and finely chopped

6 spring onions, trimmed and finely chopped

½ small green chilli, finely chopped

2 tablespoons finely chopped fresh coriander

1 tablespoon olive oil

1 dessertspoon white wine vinegar

1 dessertspoon finely chopped preserved lemon

½ teaspoon ground cumin

¼ teaspoon paprika

1 garlic clove, crushed

black pepper

shredded lettuce leaves

finely chopped fresh parsley

Soak the lentils in water for an hour, drain and put them in a pan of fresh water. Bring to the boil, cover and simmer for 30-35 minutes until tender, then drain again and rinse under cold water. Put the lentils in a mixing bowl with the tomato, chilli, coriander, preserved lemon and half of the spring onions. Steam the courgette for a few minutes to soften, then refresh under cold running water and add to the salad. Mix the oil with the vinegar, cumin, paprika and garlic and season with black pepper, pour over the salad and combine thoroughly. Arrange some shredded lettuce on a serving plate and pile the salad on top. Garnish with the remaining spring onions and some fresh parsley.

POTATO AND PARSLEY SALAD (SERVES 4)

1½lb/675g potatoes, peeled

4 spring onions, trimmed and finely sliced

3 rounded tablespoons finely chopped fresh parsley

1 tablespoon olive oil

1 tablespoon lemon juice

1 garlic clove, crushed

black pepper

Boil or steam the potatoes, then drain and allow to cool. Dice them and place them in a large bowl with the spring onions. Mix the parsley with the olive oil, lemon juice and garlic. Add to the potatoes, season with black pepper and toss well. Spoon the salad into a serving dish and either serve at room temperature or refrigerate until cold.

COUSCOUS SALAD (SERVES 4/6)

4oz/100g couscous

4oz/100g cooked sweetcorn kernels

4oz/100g cooked blackeye beans

2oz/50g cucumber, finely chopped

1oz/25g pistachio nuts, chopped

4 spring onions, trimmed and finely chopped

8 fl.oz/225ml hot vegetable stock

2 tablespoons olive oil

1 garlic clove, crushed

2 rounded tablespoons finely chopped fresh parsley

1 dessertspoon lemon juice

¼ teaspoon turmeric

black pepper

cherry tomatoes

Dissolve the turmeric in the stock and add the couscous, cover and leave for 10 minutes until the liquid has been absorbed. Add the sweetcorn, beans, cucumber, pistachios, spring onions and parsley, season with black pepper and stir well. Combine the olive oil with the garlic and lemon juice and add to the salad, mixing thoroughly. Serve garnished with quartered cherry tomatoes.

MINTED HARICOT AND BROAD BEAN SALAD (SERVES 4)

1lb/450g shelled broad beans

4oz/100g cooked haricot beans

2oz/50g tomato, skinned and chopped

4 spring onions, trimmed and finely sliced

1 garlic clove, crushed

1 tablespoon olive oil

1 dessertspoon lemon juice

2 teaspoons dried mint, crumbled

black pepper

rocket leaves

fresh mint leaves

Steam the broad beans until tender, rinse under cold running water and remove the skins. Put the broad beans in a mixing bowl with the haricot beans, tomato and spring onions. Mix the garlic with the oil, lemon juice and dried mint, season with black pepper and add to the salad. Toss very well, then keep in the fridge until cold. Arrange some rocket leaves on a serving plate, pile the bean salad on top and garnish with fresh mint leaves.

ROASTED PEPPER AND TOMATO SALAD (SERVES 4)

1¼lb/550g mixed peppers

8oz/225g tomatoes, skinned and finely chopped

1 dessertspoon olive oil

1 dessertspoon lemon juice

1 rounded teaspoon harissa

black pepper

1 tablespoon capers, chopped

finely chopped fresh coriander

Grill the peppers until the skins blister all over, allow to cool slightly and then remove the skins, stalks, membranes and seeds. Chop the pepper flesh and put it in a bowl. Drain the tomatoes and add them to the peppers. Combine the olive oil with the lemon juice and harissa and add, together with the capers. Season with black pepper and mix well, then spoon the salad into a serving bowl, cover and chill. Garnish with chopped coriander before serving.

GREEN SALAD (SERVES 4)

1 bowl of mixed leaves (e.g. rocket, baby spinach, crisp lettuce, parsley, coriander)

1 garlic clove, crushed

2 dessertspoons olive oil

1 teaspoon white wine vinegar

1 teaspoon lemon juice

pinch of cayenne pepper

black pepper

chopped pistachios

Mix the garlic with the oil, vinegar, lemon juice and cayenne pepper, season with black pepper and spoon over the leaves. Toss thoroughly and serve garnished with chopped pistachios.

SPICED BROAD BEAN AND CORN SALAD (SERVES 4)

1lb/450g shelled broad beans

8oz/225g sweetcorn kernels

4 spring onions, trimmed and finely sliced

4oz/100g tomato, skinned and finely chopped

1 garlic clove, crushed

2 dessertspoons olive oil

1 dessertspoon lemon juice

1 teaspoon ground cumin

½ teaspoon paprika

black pepper

2 tablespoons finely chopped fresh coriander

Steam the broad beans, rinse them under cold water, carefully remove the skins and put the beans in a mixing bowl with the spring onions, tomato and half of the coriander. Cook the sweetcorn and rinse it under cold running water, drain well and add. Mix the olive oil with the lemon juice, cumin, paprika and garlic, season with black pepper and spoon over the salad. Toss well and transfer to a serving bowl. Cover and refrigerate until cold, then garnish with the remaining coriander.

ORANGE, CARROT AND RADISH SALAD (SERVES 4)

2 oranges

8oz/225g carrots, scraped and grated

12 radishes, thinly sliced

2 rounded tablespoons finely chopped fresh coriander

2 dessertspoons olive oil

fresh orange juice

pinch of ground cinnamon

black pepper

finely grated orange peel

Peel the oranges and remove the pith, membranes and pips. Chop the segments and drain and keep the juice. Put the chopped orange in a large bowl with the carrots, radishes and coriander. Make up the juice with fresh orange juice to 2 dessertspoonfuls if necessary and mix with the olive oil and the cinnamon. Season with black pepper and pour over the salad. Combine well, then transfer to a serving bowl and garnish with finely grated orange peel. Cover and chill before serving.

MIXED BEAN SALAD (SERVES 4)

8oz/225g cooked mixed beans

8oz/225g French beans, topped, tailed and cut into ½ inch/1cm lengths

8oz/225g shelled broad beans

8 black olives, chopped

4 spring onions, trimmed and finely sliced

1 garlic clove, crushed

2 tablespoons finely chopped fresh coriander

2 dessertspoons olive oil

1 dessertspoon balsamic vinegar

½ teaspoon paprika

½ teaspoon ground cumin

black pepper

Steam the French beans and the broad beans separately, rinse them under cold running water and remove the skins from the broad beans. Put them in a mixing bowl with the cooked mixed beans, olives and spring onions. Combine the olive oil with the vinegar, garlic, paprika and cumin and season with black pepper. Add to the salad with half of the coriander, toss well and spoon into a serving bowl. Garnish with the remaining coriander, cover and refrigerate.

ALGERIAN CARROT AND PINE KERNEL SALAD (SERVES 4)

1lb/450g carrots, scraped and cut into thin julienne strips

1 garlic clove, crushed

2 tablespoons olive oil

1 teaspoon cumin seeds

½ teaspoon cayenne pepper

black pepper

2 dessertspoons lemon juice

2 tablespoons water

1oz/25g pine kernels, toasted

Fry the carrot, garlic, cumin seeds and cayenne pepper in the oil for 5 minutes. Add the lemon juice and water and season with black pepper, then raise the heat and cook for 5 minutes until the liquid has been absorbed. Allow to cool, spoon into a bowl and keep in the fridge until cold. Stir in the pine kernels before serving.

MEDITERRANEAN SALAD (SERVES 4)

6oz/175g aubergine, diced

4oz/100g courgette, diced

4oz/100g tomato, skinned and chopped

4oz/100g yellow pepper, chopped

4oz/100g red pepper, chopped

1 small red onion, peeled

2 garlic cloves, crushed

6 black olives, chopped

1 rounded tablespoon finely chopped fresh oregano

1 rounded tablespoon finely chopped fresh marjoram

1 tablespoon olive oil

1 teaspoon lemon juice

black pepper

rocket leaves

Steam the aubergine until tender and put in a bowl. Steam the courgette to soften slightly, then add to the aubergine together with the drained tomato, yellow and red peppers, olives, oregano and marjoram. Cut a few rings from the onion for garnish, chop the rest finely and add to the salad. Mix the garlic with the olive oil and lemon juice, season with black pepper, pour over the salad and toss very well. Cover and refrigerate until cold. Arrange some rocket leaves on a serving plate, spoon the salad on top and garnish with the onion rings.

BREAD AND TOMATO SALAD (SERVES 4)

2 pitta breads, diced

8oz/225g tomatoes, skinned and finely chopped

4oz/100g red pepper, finely chopped

4oz/100g cucumber, finely chopped

4 spring onions, trimmed and finely sliced

2 garlic cloves, crushed

6 black olives, chopped

2 rounded tablespoons finely chopped fresh parsley

2 rounded tablespoons finely chopped fresh coriander

2 rounded tablespoons finely chopped fresh mint

2 tablespoons water

2 tablespoons olive oil

1 dessertspoon lemon juice

black pepper

Sprinkle the water over the pitta bread, cover and leave for 30 minutes, then stir in the tomatoes, red pepper, cucumber, spring onions and olives. Mix the garlic with the olive oil and lemon juice and add to the salad with the herbs. Season with black pepper and toss well before serving.

BROWN LENTIL SALAD (SERVES 4)

4oz/100g brown lentils

4oz/100g aubergine, diced

4oz/100g red pepper, finely chopped

1oz/25g sultanas

2 spring onions, trimmed and finely sliced

1 garlic clove, crushed

1 tablespoon olive oil

1 rounded tablespoon finely chopped fresh coriander

1 teaspoon lemon juice

½ teaspoon ground cumin

¼ teaspoon ground cinnamon

black pepper

2 tablespoons plain soya yoghurt

shredded crisp lettuce

coriander leaves

Cook the lentils, then drain and rinse under cold running water. Drain well and put in a mixing bowl with the red pepper, sultanas, spring onions and chopped coriander. Steam the aubergine until done, rinse under cold water and add. Combine the garlic with the oil, lemon juice, cumin and cinnamon, season with black pepper and add to the bowl together with the yoghurt. Mix thoroughly, then cover and chill. Arrange some shredded lettuce on a serving plate and pile the salad on top. Garnish with coriander leaves.

ORANGE AND OLIVE SALAD (SERVES 4)

2 large oranges

12 black olives, halved

1 tablespoon olive oil

1 garlic clove, crushed

½ teaspoon paprika

¼ teaspoon ground cumin

black pepper

shredded crisp lettuce leaves

finely chopped fresh coriander

Peel the oranges and remove the pith, membranes and pips. Drain the juice off into a small bowl and arrange the orange segments and olives on a bed of shredded lettuce on a serving plate. Mix the oil, garlic, paprika and cumin with 1 tablespoonful of the orange juice, season with black pepper and whisk well. Spoon the dressing over the salad and garnish with chopped coriander.

SAUCES, DRESSINGS AND CONDIMENTS

Of all North African spice mixtures, harissa, a hot chilli-based paste, is perhaps the best known. It is widely used in Moroccan, Tunisian and Algerian cuisine in various ways, which include adding it to soups, stews and sauces for flavouring or spreading it on bread as a spicy topping. It is also mixed with plain yoghurt and served as a dip, or thinned and made into a table sauce for spooning over cooked dishes.

Charmoulas are Moroccan marinades, which can be used to marinate vegetables before grilling or baking. Preserved lemons add a fragrant lemony flavour to savoury dishes or are simply served as a garnish or separately as a condiment. Cooling yoghurt-based dressings are commonly served in all North African countries as side dishes to be spooned over hot and cold foods.

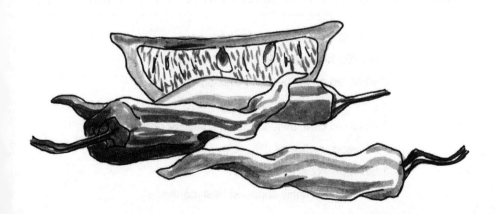

HARISSA

1oz/25g red chillies, deseeded and chopped

2 garlic cloves, chopped

1 tablespoon chopped fresh coriander

1 teaspoon coriander seeds, crushed

1 teaspoon cumin seeds, crushed

1 dessertspoon olive oil

black pepper

Blend all the ingredients together until a paste is formed. To store harissa, spoon it into a small lidded jar and just cover the top with olive oil. Store in the fridge for up to 2 weeks.

HARISSA TABLE SAUCE

2 tablespoons harissa

1 tablespoon olive oil

1 tablespoon lemon juice

1 tablespoon water

Mix the ingredients until well combined.

RED PEPPER, TOMATO AND CHILLI SAUCE (SERVES 4)

8oz/225g red pepper, finely chopped

8oz/225g tomatoes, skinned and chopped

1 small red onion, peeled and finely chopped

2 garlic cloves, crushed

1 small red chilli, deseeded and finely chopped

1 tablespoon olive oil

1 tablespoon balsamic vinegar

2 tablespoons finely chopped fresh coriander

½ teaspoon paprika

black pepper

Fry the red pepper, onion, garlic and chilli in the oil for 10 minutes, then add the remaining ingredients and combine well. Cover and simmer gently for 5-10 minutes, stirring regularly, until the sauce thickens.

PRESERVED LEMONS

unwaxed lemons

sea salt

fresh lemon juice

Cut the lemons into quarters lengthwise, to within ½ inch/1cm of the bottom of each one (in other words, the quarters are still attached to each other and an opening has been created). Fill the centre of each lemon with as much sea salt as it will hold. Squeeze the lemons back together and pack them tightly in a sterilised jar, cover with lemon juice and seal the jar. Store in a cool place for 4 weeks. To use the lemons discard the pulp and wash the peel thoroughly before chopping or slicing it.

SPICED TOMATO SAUCE (SERVES 4)

12oz/350g ripe tomatoes, skinned and chopped

1 tablespoon harissa

1 dessertspoon olive oil

1 dessertspoon tomato purée

6 spring onions, trimmed and finely chopped

black pepper

Fry the spring onions in the oil until softened. Add the remaining ingredients and stir well, then cook gently, stirring and mashing the tomatoes with the back of a spoon, for about 10 minutes until the sauce is smooth and thickens.

LEMON AND HERB CHARMOULA (SERVES 4)

2 rounded tablespoons chopped fresh thyme

2 rounded tablespoons chopped fresh parsley

2 rounded tablespoons chopped fresh coriander

4 spring onions, trimmed and chopped

2 tablespoons olive oil

2 dessertspoons lemon juice

1 dessertspoon white wine vinegar

black pepper

Put the ingredients in a blender and blend until smooth.

SPICED GARLIC CHARMOULA (SERVES 4)

4 garlic cloves, chopped

4 spring onions, trimmed and chopped

½ small red chilli, chopped

2 tablespoons olive oil

2 tablespoons chopped fresh coriander

1 dessertspoon lemon juice

½ teaspoon ground cumin

½ teaspoon paprika

black pepper

Blend the ingredients smooth.

CUCUMBER, YOGHURT AND CORIANDER DRESSING (SERVES 4)

6 fl.oz/175ml plain soya yoghurt

4oz/100g cucumber, grated and drained

2 rounded tablespoons finely chopped fresh coriander

1 garlic clove, crushed

black pepper

Mix all the ingredients well and chill before serving.

AVOCADO, PARSLEY AND GARLIC DRESSING (SERVES 4)

1 small ripe avocado, peeled and stoned

6 fl.oz/175ml plain soya yoghurt

1 dessertspoon lemon juice

4 tablespoons finely chopped fresh parsley

1 garlic clove, crushed

black pepper

Mash the avocado with the lemon juice until smooth, combine well with the rest of the ingredients and chill.

DESSERTS

Citrus fruits, dates and figs may be the best known fruits to be exported from North Africa, but many others are grown in the fertile Nile valley in Egypt and in the coastal regions along the Mediterranean. They include bananas, melons, peaches, plums, grapes, mangoes, apples and pears and all of these are regularly used to make fruit salads, which are distinctively flavoured with spices and flower waters.

Sweet pastries (see the baking section) can also make ideal desserts. Filo pastry is a particular favourite in all the countries and in Tunisia spiced mixtures of dried fruits are wrapped in individual pieces of filo pastry and fried in sunflower oil until golden brown.

DRIED FRUIT AND ORANGE SALAD (SERVES 4)

> 6oz/175g mixed dried fruit (e.g. apricot, fig, prune, peach, pear, apple), chopped
>
> 1 inch/2.5cm cinnamon stick
>
> 2 oranges
>
> 1oz/25g dried dates, chopped
>
> 6 fl.oz/175ml fresh orange juice
>
> 1 tablespoon orange flower water
>
> plain soya yoghurt
>
> chopped pistachio nuts

Put the mixed dried fruit, cinnamon stick and orange juice in a pan, cover and leave to soak for 30 minutes. Bring to the boil and simmer gently for 10-15 minutes, until the fruit is plumped up and soft. Remove the cinnamon stick and add the dates and orange flower water, then transfer to a bowl, cover and refrigerate until cold. Peel the oranges, remove the pith, membranes and pips and chop the segments. Add to the other fruit and divide the fruit salad between 4 serving bowls. Top with yoghurt and garnish with chopped pistachios.

CHERRY AND ALMOND PUDDINGS (SERVES 4)

> 8oz/225g cherries, stoned and halved
>
> 1oz/25g ground almonds
>
> 1oz/25g semolina
>
> ½oz/15g demerara sugar
>
> 12 fl.oz/350ml soya milk
>
> 1 teaspoon almond essence
>
> flaked almonds

Divide the cherries between 4 ovenproof dessert dishes. Put the ground almonds, semolina, sugar, soya milk and almond essence in a saucepan and whisk until no lumps remain. Bring to the boil, stirring all the time, and continue stirring for a minute or so until the mixture thickens, then pour it over the cherries in the dishes. Sprinkle flaked almonds on top and bake in a preheated oven at 180°C/350°F/Gas mark 4 for 15-18 minutes until golden. Serve warm.

NECTARINE- AND DATE-STUFFED PANCAKES (SERVES 4)

pancakes

4oz/100g plain flour

1oz/25g soya flour

1 rounded teaspoon ground cinnamon

12 fl.oz/350ml soya milk

vegan margarine

filling

1¼lb/550g nectarines, stoned and chopped

1oz/25g dried dates, finely chopped

½-1oz/15-25g demerara sugar (depending on ripeness of nectarines)

2 tablespoons fresh orange juice

¼ teaspoon ground cloves

to finish

orange flower water

demerara sugar

Whisk the two flours and the cinnamon with the soya milk until smooth. Cover and chill for 2 hours. Whisk again, then make eight 7 inch/18cm pancakes. Keep the pancakes warm while making the filling.

Put all the filling ingredients in a saucepan and cook gently while stirring, until the nectarines begin to soften and the mixture thickens. Divide the filling between the pancakes, rolling each one up to enclose. Sprinkle with orange flower water and demerara sugar before serving.

GINGERED MELON FRUIT SALAD (SERVES 4)

1 small charentais melon, diced and chilled

2oz/50g dried apricots, finely chopped

1oz/25g sultanas

6 fl.oz/175ml fresh orange juice

¼ teaspoon ground ginger

1oz/25g dried dates, finely chopped

2 pieces of stem ginger, finely chopped

1 tablespoon orange flower water

soya yoghurt or ice cream

Put the apricots, sultanas, orange juice and ground ginger in a small pan and bring to the boil. Cover and simmer for 5 minutes, then pour into a lidded container and add the dates, stem ginger and orange flower water. Mix thoroughly, cover and keep in the fridge until cold. Before serving stir in the diced melon until well combined, then spoon into serving bowls and top with yoghurt or ice cream.

SPICED APRICOT AND PEAR SALAD (SERVES 4)

12oz/350g fresh apricots

12oz/350g firm dessert pears

1oz/25g demerara sugar

3 tablespoons fresh orange juice

8 cloves

¼ teaspoon ground cinnamon

soya yoghurt or ice cream

Stone and chop the apricots and peel, core and chop the pears. Put in a pan with the remaining ingredients apart from the yoghurt or ice cream and stir well. Cook the fruit, stirring occasionally, for 5-6 minutes until just soft. Refrigerate until cold, then remove the cloves and serve topped with yoghurt or ice cream.

ALMOND AND RAISIN RICE (SERVES 4)

2oz/50g ground rice

1oz/25g ground almonds

1oz/25g raisins

1oz/25g demerara sugar

1 rounded dessertspoon vegan margarine

20 fl.oz/600ml soya milk

1 teaspoon almond essence

toasted flaked almonds

Bring the soya milk to the boil with the raisins and almond essence, then remove from the heat. Melt the margarine in another pan and stir in the ground rice. Take off the cooker and add the ground almonds and sugar and the raisins and soya milk, mixing very well to ensure that no lumps remain. Return the pan to the stove and bring to the boil while stirring constantly. Lower the heat and continue stirring for a minute or so until the mixture thickens, but be careful because it tends to spit out of the pan at this stage. Spoon the mixture into 4 serving bowls, cover and put in the fridge. Serve cold, garnished with flaked almonds.

BANANA AND RAISIN COUSCOUS (SERVES 4)

1 large ripe banana

10 fl.oz/300ml plain soya yoghurt

2oz/50g couscous

5 fl.oz/150ml soya milk

1oz/25g raisins

½ oz/15g demerara sugar

½ teaspoon ground cinnamon

chopped pistachios

Bring the raisins, sugar, cinnamon and soya milk to the boil, then remove from the heat and add the couscous. Stir well, cover and leave for 15 minutes. Stir the couscous to break it up and put in the fridge to get cold. Peel and chop the banana and add it to the couscous together with the yoghurt. Mix until well combined, then divide between 4 glasses and garnish with chopped pistachios.

DATE- AND ALMOND-STUFFED BAKED PEACHES (SERVES 4)

4 large peaches, halved and stoned

2oz/50g dried dates, finely chopped

1oz/25g ground almonds

3 fl.oz/75ml fresh orange juice

orange flower water

toasted flaked almonds

soya yoghurt

Put the dates and orange juice in a small pan and bring to the boil. Simmer gently, stirring all the while and mashing the dates with the back of a spoon, until thick and smooth. Remove from the heat and add the ground almonds. Make the hollows in the peach halves a bit bigger by removing some of the flesh, chop this finely and add it to the date and almond mixture. Combine well, then fill each peach half with some of the mixture, shaping it into a mound on top. Place them in a greased baking dish and sprinkle with orange flower water. Bake in a preheated oven at 180°C/350°F/Gas mark 4 for about 25 minutes until cooked. Garnish with flaked almonds and serve topped with yoghurt.

BAKED SEMOLINA AND PEACH PUDDING (SERVES 4)

8oz/225g peaches, stoned and chopped

1½oz/40g semolina

1oz/25g demerara sugar

1 dessertspoon vegan margarine

15 fl.oz/450ml soya milk

¼ teaspoon ground cinnamon

rose flower water

extra ground cinnamon

Arrange the peaches in a greased 7 inch/18cm round ovenproof dish and sprinkle with rose flower water. Melt the margarine and stir in the semolina, sugar and ¼ teaspoon of cinnamon. Remove from the heat and add the soya milk, then whisk smooth and return to the heat. Bring to the boil while stirring constantly, then pour the mixture over the peaches in the dish and bake in a preheated oven at 180°C/350°F/Gas mark 4 for 25-30 minutes until golden brown. Sprinkle with cinnamon and serve either at room temperature or chilled.

BANANA AND GINGER PANCAKES (SERVES 4)

12oz/350g bananas, peeled and lightly mashed

10 fl.oz/300ml soya milk

4oz/100g plain flour

2 teaspoons ground ginger

vegan margarine

lemon juice

1 rounded teaspoon demerara sugar

½ teaspoon ground ginger

Mix the demerara sugar with the ½ teaspoon ground ginger. Whisk the flour and the 2 teaspoons ground ginger with the soya milk until smooth, add the banana and mix thoroughly. Heat a little margarine in a 6 inch/15cm non-stick frying pan until hot and make 8 pancakes, using 2 tablespoonfuls of batter for each one. Keep the pancakes warm until they are all made, then roll them up and sprinkle them with lemon juice and a little of the sugar and ginger mixture.

BAKING

Cakes, biscuits and pastries are enjoyed as snacks at any time of the day in all North African countries and they are usually accompanied by mint tea or strong black coffee. Similar recipes are used all over the region and popular ingredients include citrus fruits, almonds, semolina, dates, walnuts and flower waters. Some products are specific to certain countries, such as gazelle's horns, which are a Moroccan speciality traditionally served at weddings. Many Egyptians are very fond of chocolate and strong black coffee and these two ingredients are combined to make a delicious, richly-flavoured cake.

ALMOND BISCUITS (MAKES APPROX. 16)

3oz/75g ground almonds

2oz/50g plain flour

2oz/50g vegan margarine

1oz/25g demerara sugar

½ teaspoon baking powder

½ teaspoon almond essence

1 tablespoon soya milk

Cream the margarine with the sugar, work in the ground almonds and almond essence, then add the sifted flour and baking powder together with the soya milk. Mix thoroughly until everything binds together. Take heaped teaspoonfuls of the mixture and roll into balls in the palm of the hand. Flatten them into thick biscuit shapes and put them on a greased baking sheet. Bake in a preheated oven at 180°C/350°F/Gas mark 4 for about 10 minutes until golden brown. Allow the biscuits to cool on the baking sheet for 5 minutes before sliding them onto a wire rack.

CINNAMON AND RAISIN DOUGHNUTS (MAKES 8)

8oz/225g plain flour

½ teaspoon salt

1 rounded teaspoon easy-blend yeast

1 teaspoon ground cinnamon

1oz/25g demerara sugar

1oz/25g raisins, chopped

approx. 5 fl.oz/150ml warm water

sunflower oil

extra ground cinnamon

Stir the flour, salt, yeast, ground cinnamon, sugar and raisins together and gradually add the water until a soft dough forms. Knead the dough well, then return to the bowl, cover and leave in a warm place for 1 hour. Knead the dough again and divide it into 8 equal pieces. Roll each piece into a ball and push a thumb through the centre to make a hole. Widen the holes, then put the doughnuts on a baking sheet and allow to rise for 30 minutes in a warm place. Shallow fry the doughnuts in hot sunflower oil for a few minutes on each side until golden. Drain on kitchen paper and sprinkle lightly with ground cinnamon. Serve warm.

EGYPTIAN CHOCOLATE CAKE

8oz/225g plain flour

3oz/75g vegan margarine

2oz/50g demerara sugar

2oz/50g vegan chocolate block, broken

4 fl.oz/125ml black coffee

2 fl.oz/50ml soya milk

1 dessertspoon baking powder

1 teaspoon vanilla essence

½ teaspoon ground cinnamon

¼ teaspoon ground cloves

2½oz/65g vegan chocolate block

Cream the margarine with the sugar in a mixing bowl. Put the broken chocolate block in a small saucepan with the coffee and heat gently until melted and combined. Add to the bowl alternately with the sifted flour, baking powder and spices, mixing well between additions. Add the soya milk and vanilla essence and combine thoroughly. Spoon the mixture into a lined and greased 7 inch/18cm round baking tin and level the top. Bake in a preheated oven at 180°C/350°F/Gas mark 4 for about 25 minutes, until a skewer comes out clean when inserted in the centre. Carefully turn out onto a wire rack and allow to cool. Grate ½oz/15g of the remaining chocolate and melt the rest in a bowl over a pan of boiling water. Spread the melted chocolate over the top and sides of the cake and sprinkle the grated chocolate on top. Refrigerate until the chocolate sets before cutting the cake into wedges.

DATE-STUFFED SEMOLINA PASTRIES (MAKES 10)

pastry

8oz/225g semolina

4oz/100g plain flour

1oz/25g sesame seeds

4 tablespoons sunflower oil

1 rounded teaspoon baking powder

5 fl.oz/150ml warm water

orange flower water

filling

8oz/225g dried dates, finely chopped

4 fl.oz/125ml fresh orange juice

½ teaspoon ground cinnamon

Sift the flour and baking powder into a large bowl, add the semolina and sesame seeds and mix. Add the oil and stir until everything is well combined and the mixture is crumbly. Gradually add the warm water to form a soft dough. Knead the dough well, return it to the bowl and leave it for 20 minutes.

Put the dates, orange juice and cinnamon in a small pan and bring to the boil. Lower the heat and cook gently while mashing the dates with the back of a spoon until thick and smooth. Remove from the heat and allow to cool. Roll out the pastry on a floured piece of cling film into an oblong of 13 x 5 inches/33 x 13cm. Spread the date mixture evenly along the centre and fold the two long sides of the pastry towards the middle, squeezing the edges together to join. Carefully transfer the pastry roll to a greased baking sheet, with the join underneath. Brush the top with orange flower water and mark it into 10 equal slices with a sharp knife. Bake in a preheated oven at 180°C/350°F/Gas mark 4 for about 20 minutes until golden brown. Cut through into slices and transfer to a wire rack to cool.

ALMOND, SULTANA AND SESAME PASTRIES (MAKES 12)

10oz/300g packet filo pastry

2oz/50g vegan margarine, melted

1oz/25g sesame seeds, toasted

filling

8oz/225g ground almonds

4oz/100g sultanas, chopped

2 tablespoons finely grated orange zest

6 tablespoons fresh orange juice

1 tablespoon orange flower water

½ teaspoon ground cinnamon

syrup

1oz/25g demerara sugar

5 fl.oz/150ml water

1 dessertspoon orange flower water

Put the sultanas, orange juice and tablespoon flower water in a lidded bowl and leave to soak for 1 hour, then mix in the almonds, orange zest and cinnamon. Cut the pastry into 24 sheets, each about 9 x 5 inches/23 x 13cm. Lay 12 sheets on a flat surface and brush with melted margarine, then place another sheet on top of each one. Divide the filling equally between the 12 oblongs, putting it at one end only. Fold the two long edges of each oblong towards the centre, then roll up to enclose the filling completely. Arrange the pastries on a greased baking sheet and brush them with the remaining melted margarine. Bake in a preheated oven at 180°C/350°F/Gas mark 4 for about 25 minutes until browned.

Towards the end of the cooking time, bring the ingredients for the syrup to the boil in a small saucepan and simmer for about 10 minutes until the mixture thickens. Dip the pastries in the syrup until covered and sprinkle them all over with toasted sesame seeds. Serve warm.

Moroccan serpent cake (serves 6)

6 sheets filo pastry of approx. 19 x 5 inches/48 x 13cm

1oz/25g vegan margarine, melted

ground cinnamon

filling

8oz/225g ground almonds

2oz/50g breadcrumbs

1oz/25g demerara sugar

1oz/25g vegan margarine, melted

1 tablespoon rose water

6 tablespoons soya milk

1 teaspoon almond essence

Melt the margarine for the filling, remove from the heat and stir in the ground almonds, sugar and breadcrumbs. Add the rose water, soya milk and almond essence and mix until a paste forms.

Put one sheet of filo pastry on a flat surface and brush with melted margarine, them place another sheet on top. Take one third of the filling and with damp hands form it into a 19 inch/48cm long roll. Arrange the roll of filling along the length of the pastry and roll this up to enclose it. Repeat this twice with the remaining ingredients to end up with 3 filled rolls. Take one of the rolls and shape it into a tight coil on a greased baking sheet. Join the second roll to the end of the first one and continue coiling, then the third one. Brush with the remaining melted margarine and bake in a preheated oven at 180°C/350°F/Gas mark 4 for about 25 minutes until golden brown. Sprinkle with ground cinnamon and serve warm, cut into wedges.

ORANGE AND APRICOT SLICES (MAKES 8)

pastry

4oz/100g plain flour

4oz/100g semolina

1 rounded teaspoon baking powder

1oz/25g demerara sugar

2 tablespoons sunflower oil

2 fl.oz/50ml fresh orange juice

finely grated zest of 1 orange

1 tablespoon orange flower water

¼ teaspoon ground cloves

filling

1 orange

4oz/100g dried apricots, finely chopped

2 fl.oz/50ml fresh orange juice

topping

½oz/15g demerara sugar

2 fl.oz/50ml fresh orange juice

Finely grate the zest from the orange. Remove all the pith, membranes and pips and finely chop the segments. Put them in a small pan with the apricots and orange juice and bring to the boil. Cover and simmer, stirring frequently, until the liquid has been absorbed and the mixture is thick. Remove from the heat and allow to cool.

Sift the flour, ground cloves and baking powder into a large bowl. Add the semolina, sugar and grated orange zest and mix. Stir in the sunflower oil and orange juice until a soft dough forms. Knead the dough well, then divide it into 2 equal pieces and roll each piece out on a floured board into a 7 inch/18cm square. Place one square in a lined and greased 7 inch/18cm square baking tin and spread the filling evenly over it, then put the other pastry square on top and press down lightly. Mark the pastry into 8 equal portions and bake in a preheated oven at 180°C/350°F/Gas mark 4 for about 25 minutes until golden. Carefully transfer to a wire rack.

Put the sugar and orange juice for the topping in a small saucepan and bring to the boil. Simmer gently until the mixture thickens, then brush it evenly over the top of the pastry. Allow to cool before cutting through into 8 slices.

SEMOLINA AND LEMON BISCUITS (MAKES APPROX. 20)

4oz/100g plain flour

2oz/50g semolina

2oz/50g vegan margarine

1oz/25g demerara sugar

finely grated zest of 1 lemon

1 teaspoon baking powder

3 tablespoons lemon juice

Melt the margarine with the sugar, then remove from the heat and add the sifted flour and baking powder, grated lemon zest and semolina. Stir well, add the lemon juice and mix until everything binds together. Take heaped teaspoonfuls of the mixture and with damp hands roll into balls. Put these on a greased baking sheet and flatten them slightly, then press the back of a fork in the top of each one and neaten the edges. Bake in a preheated oven at 180°C/350°F/Gas mark 4 for 12-15 minutes until golden. Leave to cool on a wire rack.

GAZELLE'S HORNS (MAKES 8)

pastry

4oz/100g plain flour

1½oz/40g vegan margarine, melted

1 teaspoon baking powder

1 tablespoon orange flower water

approx. 2 tablespoons soya milk

extra soya milk

filling

2oz/50g ground almonds

½oz/15g vegan margarine, melted

½oz/15g demerara sugar

¼ teaspoon ground cinnamon

1 dessertspoon orange flower water

Sift the flour and baking powder into a bowl and mix in the melted margarine and orange flower water. Gradually add the soya milk until a soft dough forms. Turn this out onto a floured board and roll it out to about ¼ inch/5mm thick. Cut the dough into eight 3 inch/8cm circles with a pastry cutter, gathering up and re-rolling as necessary.

Mix the filling ingredients into a paste and divide the mixture between the 8 pastry circles, placing it on one half of each circle only. Dampen the edges with soya milk and fold the pastry over to enclose the filling. Press the edges together with a fork and form the half-circles into crescent shapes before putting them on a greased baking sheet. Brush the tops with soya milk and bake in a preheated oven at 180°C/350°F/Gas mark 4 for about 12 minutes until browned. Cool on a wire rack.

CINNAMON, DATE AND ORANGE CAKE

6oz/175g plain flour

4oz/100g dried dates, finely chopped

2oz/50g semolina

2oz/50g vegan margarine

2oz/50g demerara sugar

8 fl.oz/225ml fresh orange juice

finely grated zest of 1 orange

1 tablespoon orange flower water

1 teaspoon baking powder

½ teaspoon ground cinnamon

topping

1 dessertspoon demerara sugar

½ teaspoon ground cinnamon

orange flower water

Cream the margarine with the sugar, add the semolina, grated orange zest and orange flower water and mix well. Stir in the dates, then add the sifted flour, baking powder and cinnamon alternately with the orange juice. Mix thoroughly, then cover and leave for 5 minutes. Spoon the mixture into a lined and greased 7 inch/18cm round baking tin and spread it out evenly. Mix the sugar and cinnamon for the topping and sprinkle over the top, pressing it in lightly with the back of a spoon. Bake in a preheated oven at 180°C/350°F/Gas mark 4 for about 30 minutes until golden brown. Carefully turn out onto a wire rack and sprinkle the top lightly with orange flower water. Allow to cool before cutting into wedges.

DATE AND WALNUT BRIOUATES (MAKES 12)

10oz/300g packet filo pastry

2oz/50g vegan margarine, melted

sesame seeds

filling

8oz/225g dried dates, finely chopped

4oz/100g walnuts, grated

4 fl.oz/125ml water

½ teaspoon ground cinnamon

¼ teaspoon ground cloves

Put the dates and water in a pan and bring to the boil. Lower the heat and cook gently while mashing the dates with the back of a spoon, until the mixture is thick and smooth. Remove from the heat and allow to cool. Add the walnuts and spices and mix thoroughly.

Cut the pastry into 24 pieces of about 10 x 5 inches/25 x 13cm. Lay 12 sheets on a flat surface and brush them with melted margarine. Put another sheet of pastry on top of each one, then divide the filling equally between the oblongs, placing it in the left hand corner. Fold the pastry over towards the right, then up and then to the left, folding the edges in as you go, to enclose the filling and make triangles. Transfer the triangles to a greased baking sheet, brush with melted margarine and sprinkle with sesame seeds, then bake in a preheated oven at 180°C/350°F/Gas mark 4 for about 25 minutes until golden. Let the briouates cool slightly before serving.

DRINKS

The drinking of mint tea is almost a ritual in most North African countries and it is served at any time of the day, both at home and in cafés and market places. It is an especially popular after-dinner drink, to aid digestion. Drinking strong black coffee, too, either plain or flavoured with spices, is traditional, especially for men meeting up with friends to play backgammon and smoke water pipes in the numerous coffee houses. Hot chocolate is a favourite drink in Egypt and is enjoyed particularly in the winter months. But when the weather is hot, cold refreshing drinks are welcome and freshly squeezed orange juice, or vegetables and fresh and dried fruits, blended with water, milk or yoghurt, are all very popular.

MINT TEA (SERVES 4)

12 mint sprigs (preferably spearmint)

4 teaspoons green tea leaves

24 fl.oz/725ml boiling water

sugar (optional)

Bruise the mint leaves to release the flavour and put them in a pot with the tea leaves and boiling water. Add sugar if desired and stir well. Leave to steep for 4 minutes before straining into cups.

ALMOND MILK (SERVES 4)

2oz/50g whole blanched almonds, finely ground

32 fl.oz/950ml soya milk

1 tablespoon demerara sugar

1 tablespoon orange flower water

Toast the ground almonds until just golden, then put in a pan and add the soya milk, sugar and orange flower water. Bring to the boil while stirring, remove from the heat, cover and leave for 5 minutes. Strain the milk through a fine sieve, pressing out as much liquid as possible with the back of a spoon. Stir before serving either warm or cold.

CARDAMOM COFFEE (SERVES 4)

24 fl.oz/725ml strong black coffee

12 cardamom pods, husked

1 rounded tablespoon demerara sugar

Lightly crush the cardamom seeds and put them in a saucepan with the coffee and sugar. Stir well and bring to the boil. Simmer for 1 minute, then remove from the heat. Cover and leave to stand for 3 minutes. Strain into cups to serve.

HOT CHOCOLATE (SERVES 4)

3oz/75g vegan chocolate bar, broken

24 fl.oz/725ml soya milk

sugar (optional)

ground cinnamon

Put the broken chocolate, soya milk and a little sugar, if wished, in a pan and stir well. Slowly bring to the boil, whisking constantly until the chocolate has melted. Pour into cups and sprinkle with ground cinnamon.

THICK AVOCADO SHAKE (SERVES 4)

1 small ripe avocado, peeled and chopped

20 fl.oz/600ml chilled soya milk

crushed ice

Blend the avocado with the soya milk until smooth, then pour into glasses and add crushed ice.

CHILLED APPLE MILK (SERVES 4)

8oz/225g apples, peeled, cored and chopped

4 tablespoons water

1 dessertspoon demerara sugar

1 dessertspoon rose flower water

20 fl.oz/600ml soya milk

crushed ice

4 apple slices

Cook the apple with the water and sugar until soft. Allow to cool, then blend with the soya milk and rose flower water. Transfer to a jug, cover and refrigerate until cold. Stir the apple milk and pour it into glasses. Add crushed ice and garnish each glass with a slice of apple.

BANANA AND CINNAMON SHAKE (SERVES 4)

12oz/350g ripe bananas, peeled and chopped

24 fl.oz/725ml chilled soya milk

1 tablespoon demerara sugar

½ teaspoon ground cinnamon

crushed ice

extra ground cinnamon

Blend the banana, soya milk, sugar and ½ teaspoonful of ground cinnamon smooth. Pour into glasses, add crushed ice and sprinkle with a little ground cinnamon.

YOGHURT AND CUCUMBER COOLER (SERVES 4)

6oz/175g cucumber, chopped

4 rounded tablespoons plain soya yoghurt

20 fl.oz/600ml water

crushed ice

4 cucumber slices

Put the chopped cucumber, yoghurt and water in a blender and blend until smooth. Keep in the fridge until cold, then pass through a sieve into a jug, pressing out as much liquid as possible with the back of a spoon. Whisk until well combined and pour into glasses, add crushed ice and garnish with a cucumber slice.

MELON AND APRICOT CRUSH (SERVES 4)

8oz/225g melon flesh, chopped

2oz/50g dried apricots, finely chopped

24 fl.oz/725ml water

melon balls

Bring the apricots and 10 fl.oz/300ml of the water to the boil in a small pan. Cover and simmer for 15 minutes, then remove from the heat and allow to cool. Transfer to a blender, add the chopped melon and remaining water, blend until smooth and chill. Whisk the juice until well combined, pour it into glasses and serve topped with melon balls.

APRICOT, APPLE AND ORANGE JUICE (SERVES 4)

2oz/50g dried apricots, chopped

10 fl.oz/300ml water

9 fl.oz/250ml fresh apple juice

9 fl.oz/250ml fresh orange juice

4 apple slices

Put the apricots and water in a saucepan and bring to the boil, cover and simmer for 10 minutes. Leave to cool, then transfer to a blender and add the apple and orange juice. Blend smooth and put in the fridge. When cold stir well, pour into 4 glasses and garnish each glass with a slice of apple.

CARROT AND ORANGE JUICE (SERVES 4)

8oz/225g carrot, scraped and chopped

10 fl.oz/300ml water

12 fl.oz/350ml chilled fresh orange juice

1 dessertspoon orange flower water

crushed ice

4 orange slices

Blend the carrot with the water until smooth, cover and refrigerate for 2 hours. Pass the juice through a sieve into a jug, pressing out as much liquid from the pulp as possible with the back of a spoon, then add the orange juice and flower water and stir well. Pour into glasses and add crushed ice. Garnish each glass with a slice of orange before serving.

TOMATO JUICE (SERVES 4)

12oz/350g ripe tomatoes, skinned and chopped

20 fl.oz/600ml water

1 dessertspoon tomato purée

1 dessertspoon demerara sugar

black pepper

Bring all the ingredients to the boil. Cover and simmer for 5 minutes until the tomatoes are soft. Allow to cool, then blend until smooth. Sieve the juice into a jug, cover and chill. Stir well before pouring into glasses.

6